MARX AND THE TRADE UNIONS

MARX

and the

TRADE UNIONS

by

A. LOZOVSKY, [pseud. for
Dridzo, Solomon Abramovich]

GREENWOOD PRESS, PUBLISHERS
WESTPORT, CONNECTICUT

Library of Congress Cataloging in Publication Data

Dridzo, Solomon Abramovich, 1878-
   Marx and the trade unions.

   Translation of Karl Marks i profsoīuzy.
   Reprint of the ed. published by International Pub-
lishers, New York.
   Includes index.
   1. Marx, Karl, 1818-1883. 2. Trade-unions and
communism. I. Title.
HX544.D713 1976   331.88'01   75-22758
ISBN 0-8371-8352-9

First published in 1935 by International Publishers, New York

Reprinted with the permission of International Publishers

Reprinted in 1976 by Greenwood Press, Inc.

Library of Congress Catalog Card Number 75-22758

ISBN 0-8371-8352-9

Printed in the United States of America

CONTENTS

PREFACE

THIS book goes beyond the scope of its title.

First of all, because it gives not only the position of Marx on the trade unions, but also that of Engels, who is second to Marx as creator of the theory, strategy and tactics of revolutionary Marxism.

Second, the tasks of the trade unions can be correctly defined only on the basis of the general class tasks of the proletariat—this leads to going beyond the framework of narrow trade union problems and to studying the political line of Marx and Engels concerning the problems of the labour movement.

Third, history is the most political and most partisan science of all sciences. To study the past without relation to the present is possible only for persons who either have no sense of party or political responsibility whatever, or whose sense of this responsibility has become completely atrophied.

There are people who believe that to be a historian or a keeper of archives is almost one and the same thing, the only difference being that the keeper of archives collects documents of the past, while the historian comments on these documents, without leaving the framework of this past. This is wrong. The historian utilises documents concerning the past, but if he fails to see things beyond the walls of his archives, if he does not leave the palisade of the past, if he fails to glance over the fence hedging off old historical dates, he considerably lessens the value of his work. The past must help our struggle to-day. Otherwise it is not worth while spending time studying it. The positive and negative experiences acquired in the past must arm us for the struggle for a better future. The task is not only to study the world, but to transform it.

This is what the author had in mind when he sat down to shed light on the trade union heritage of Marx and Engels. After having thoroughly analysed the views of Marx and Engels in the field of the trade union movement and economic struggle, I

7

realised clearly that we were late, that we should not have waited for the 50th anniversary of the death of Marx, but should long ago have collected all the views of Marx and Engels on the trade union movement and the economic struggle of the working class. Indeed, we are late. However, better late than never.

Marx and Engels are modern; they are modern not only in what they themselves wrote, but in what their successors, their best pupils, have been doing since their departure from the battlefield. This means that we must study carefully what Lenin and Stalin contributed to the problem of immediate interest to us. That is why the author considers this book to be only a beginning. The second part will be *Lenin and the Trade Unions,* the third part, *Stalin and the Trade Unions,* while all three parts together will constitute *Revolutionary Marxism and the Trade Union Movement.* This work must include not only the pre-war experience of the socialist and trade union internationals, but also the experience of the Marxian experience of the Communist International and the Red International of Labour Unions. It was time, high time, that this work was started. I hope that our strong historians will be drawn into the task and that all will jointly succeed in working out the theory, strategy and tactics of Marx, Engels, Lenin and Stalin in the trade union movement.

If this book will serve as an impetus, as a starting-point in furthering this great and complicated task of making a Marxian analysis of the theoretical and tactical principles of the international revolutionary trade union movement, its publication will have been justified.

A. L.

Moscow, March 14, 1933.

INTRODUCTION

As the physical image of Karl Marx fades more and more into the past, the spiritual figure of this giant of thought and revolutionary action comes more and more vividly to the fore. Marx represents a whole world of ideas and images; he is unsurpassed as a theoretician, statesman, strategist and tactician of the class struggle. His brain was like a tremendous laboratory, which analytically and synthetically worked over facts and events, beginning with revolutions, wars, colonial revolts, pronunciamentos, peasant rebellions and parliamentary debates, and ending with strikes, demonstrations and even the smallest spontaneous economic and political actions.

Marx was not merely a person of encyclopædic education, he was an independent dialectic thinker. He was not a scientist in the narrow, professorial sense of the word. He was an innovator, bold to the extreme, who fearlessly carried his thoughts to their logical conclusion. He was one of those thinkers (and there have been very few of them in the history of mankind) who with the minds of great geniuses looked into the future, and with the daring hands of revolutionaries and artists ("my work represents one artistic whole," he wrote to Engels in 1865) pointed out the path of development from capitalism to communism.

Marx did not guess nor did he prophesy. He argued, analysed, dissected facts, exposed their inner connections and placed them in such a way that they themselves compelled definite conclusions. He placed Hegelian dialectics on its feet, he was never lost in the face of facts; always remaining firm, he knew exactly what he wanted in theory, in politics and in tactics.

Marx devoured an enormous number of books, deeply analysed facts and moulded them with his masterful mind, which to the very last days of his life continued to pour forth ever-new treasures for the international proletariat.

9

Marx was not a dry bookworm; he seethed with the great passion and ardour of a fighter. He disliked unnecessary words, glib but empty phrases, and fought against those who roamed in the "misty realm of philosophical phantasy" (*Communist Manifesto,* p. 32). Every phrase written by Marx, every one of his words lives to-day—so much life and passion is there in the works of this great scientist, the tireless destroyer of all pseudo-scientific authorities, the exposer of petty-bourgeois babblers, the merciless enemy of all pseudo-socialist schools, sects and groupings.

Marx did not like words devoid of content, phrases without deeds; physically he could not tolerate phrasemongers of socialism. His mind penetrated to the very essence of a question. He knew how to extract the main issues, the very essence from the tens of thousands of pages that he had read and from the hundreds of thousands of facts he had stored up; he was able to say much in few words.

Marx possessed the special ability of clothing his rich thought in scant but vivid language. This is why even to-day when one immerses oneself in the works of Marx one is bound to feel deeply moved. It is not only his major works that have retained their importance up to the present time; even his separate articles on vital questions, his notes and letters going far back to the nineteenth century, throw light on the path of the development of the labour movement in the twentieth century. The more one peruses the rich inheritance of Marx, the more vital it becomes, the more pronounced become the features of this great theoretician and organiser of the working class, the nearer and more comprehensible does he grow—he who gave his life for the purpose of converting the working class "from a class for others into a class for itself."

Marx is multiform, but uniform and consistent in all that he said and did. Not in vain did he succinctly describe the distinguishing feature of his character as *singleness of purpose*. Only conditionally is it possible to separate some one question or group of questions from the whole of Marx's work. However, it must be borne in mind at the outset that the inheritance that Marx left is the richest that any person ever left to his descendants, that it is monolithic and it is difficult to divide into separate parts.

It is especially difficult to separate from the depository of ideas and thoughts that Marx left that part which deals with the trade union movement and the economic struggle. Marx did not write any special books or pamphlet or textbook on this subject. His ideas on problems of the economic struggle and the *rôle* of the trade unions in the past, present and future can be found all through his works, especially in his practical work as leader of the International Workingmen's Association.

Is it worth while to collect the opinions and ideas of Marx on questions of the trade unions? Has he, admirers of textbooks and thick reference works might ask, a definite opinion on these problems? To this we can reply—*indeed, it is worth while.* The slightest, if serious, acquaintance with the works of Marx shows that although Marx did not write any thick books on the trade unions and although he did not frequently deal with this question, still *the separate opinions expressed by him constitute a definite system, map out a definite line and give an absolutely definite understanding of the rôle and tasks of the trade unions in the general class struggle of the proletariat.* It must be borne in mind that in these questions Marx also laid out new roads. The three sources of Marxism mentioned by Lenin (classical German philosophy, classical English political economy and French socialism) had to be mastered by Marx.

Marx first and foremost was thoroughly conversant with the sciences of his period. He built his teachings on the "solid foundation of human knowledge acquired under capitalism." After having studied the laws of the development of human society, Marx

realised the inevitability of the development of capitalism leading to communism, and, what is most important, he proved this solely on the basis of the most exact, most detailed and most thorough study of this capitalist society, by completely mastering all that former sciences could give. All that had been created he analysed critically, not omitting a single point. All that the human mind had created he worked over, subjected to criticism, tested in the labour movement and drew conclusions that people with a limited bourgeois outlook, hidebound by bourgeois prejudices, could not draw. (Lenin.)

Marx was distinguished for his exceptional scientific conscientiousness, and in view of the fact that he had excellently mastered the method of dialectic materialism, his scientific works represent a splendid example of *scientific foresight*. Marx followed the first steps of the trade union movement in England, France and Germany, saw its strong and weak points, thought a great deal about all that was happening, found out just what the trade unions were, what were the limits of their action, what were the relations between economics and politics. He did all this with the accuracy, profundity and clarity so characteristic of him.

The basic idea in Marx's conception of the economic struggle of the working class was the necessity of turning the working class into a class for itself, drawing the line between the working class and the bourgeoisie, uniting the working class, consolidating its forces, setting up the working class against the bourgeoisie. This idea is woven like a red thread into the entire texture of Marx's writings and actions. It was also this idea that defined his point of view on the trade unions, the tasks confronting them and their *rôle* in the general class struggle of the proletariat.

But to turn the working class into a class for itself is possible only when the masses begin to understand the theory and tactics of the class struggle. Marx himself says that he did not invent the theory of the class struggle. In his letter to Weydemeyer, dated March 5, 1852, Marx writes:

> What was new on my part was to prove the following: (1) that the existence of classes is connected only with definite historical phases in the development of production; (2) that the class struggle necessarily leads to the dictatorship of the proletariat; (3) that this dictatorship is itself only a transition to the abolition of all classes and to a classless society.

The merit of Marx consists further in the fact that he placed the theory of the class struggle on a firm economic basis, that from his economic analyses he drew political and tactical conclusions, that he waged a merciless struggle against all attempts to erect a bridge between classes, to screen the gulf between the bourgeoisie and the proletariat and to turn the working class ideologically and politically into an auxiliary weapon of the bourgeoisie.

Marx worked out the theory of wages, discovered the theory of surplus value, smashed the bourgeois, petty-bourgeois and semi-socialist theories (Adam Smith, Ricardo, Mill, Proudhon, Lassalle, etc.) concerning the price of labour, the proportional increase of prices of products in accordance with increases in wages, the iron law of wages, etc., *and in this way created an economic and political basis for building class trade unions and a class trade union policy.*

Further, Marx's merits consist not only in the fact that he saw and exposed the class line that separates the proletariat from the bourgeoisie, but that he forged a theoretical and political weapon by means of which he found it possible consistently to defend this class position.

"Marx was before all else a revolutionary," Engels said at Marx's grave.[1] He was a revolutionary not only in philosophy, history and economics; he was a revolutionary in politics and tactics. With all his passion for books and original sources (his favourite pastime, as he himself declared, was to burrow in books), Marx would always lay aside his theoretical works the moment he was confronted with the slightest possibility for political action. He could not imagine life without a strenuous, passionate struggle for his views and principles. To the question: "What is your idea of happiness?" he replied: "To struggle." It is precisely this feature that Engels particularly stressed in his funeral oration. "Marx was before all else a revolutionary," he said.

His real mission in life was to contribute in one way or another to the overthrow of capitalist society and of the forms of government which it had brought into being, *to contribute to the liberation of the present-day proletariat, which he was the first to make conscious of its own position and its needs, of the conditions under which it could win its freedom. Fighting was his element. And he fought with a passion, a tenacity and a success such as few could rival.*

Marx combined in himself the outstanding theoretician and the great revolutionary. His life vocation was to rouse the oppressed against the oppressors. This vocation he expressed in the terse but incisive phrase: *"I am a mortal enemy of capitalism."*

Trade Union problems do not occupy very much space in the vast Marxian heritage. However, here just as in other questions,

[1] March 17, 1883. *The Fourteenth of March*, Martin Lawrence, Ltd.

we have every reason to examine carefully just what Marx did say. His distinction lies not only in the fact that he said something new in his time, but also in the fact that whatever was new in what he said is still applicable even on the fiftieth anniversary of his death. That is why Engels was right when he said that Marx's name and his cause will survive the ages.

CHAPTER I

Rôle of the Trade Unions in the General Class Struggle of the Proletariat

MARX began to think politically in the epoch when trade unions had just come into being. He became a Communist at a time when in some countries the trade unions had only begun to crystallise out of various mutual aid societies (France), while in other countries (England) the trade unions waged economic strikes and struggles for the right of suffrage. He found only embryonic forms of organisation, extremely primitive, variegated in their ideology and composition, bearing all the birthmarks of their origin. The greatness of Marx consists precisely in the fact that he realised that this represented only the first steps of the infant working class and that it was impossible to judge the historical rôle of the given organisation and the path of its development from these primitive forms of the movement.

Marx, first and foremost, considered the trade unions *organising centres*, centres for collecting the forces of the workers, organisations for giving the workers an elementary class training. What was most important for Marx? The fact that *the scattered workers, competing with one another, were now beginning to close their ranks and come out jointly.* In this he saw a guarantee that the working class would develop into an independent power. Marx and Engels repeatedly refer in their works to the idea that the trade unions are schools of solidarity, schools of socialism. A great deal is said on this question, particularly in their correspondence, where a number of questions which they could not raise in the international social press in view of the low level of the movement were raised more frankly and sharply.

The trade unions are schools of socialism. But Marx does not confine himself to formulas. He develops his idea, he approaches

15

the problem of trade unions from all angles. Karl Marx was the author of the resolution on the question of the past, present and future of the trade unions, adopted at the Geneva Congress of the First International. What, then, is the past of the trade unions?

Capital is concentrated social power, while the worker has only his individual labour power at his disposal. Therefore the agreement between Capital and Labour can never be based on just terms, just not even in the sense of a society that places on one side the possession of the material means of life and production, and on the opposite side sets down the live productive forces. The only social force possessed by the workers is their numerical strength. This force, however, is impaired by the absence of unity. The lack of unity among the workers is caused by the inevitable competition among themselves, and is maintained by it. *The trade unions developed originally out of the spontaneous attempts of the workers to do away with this competition, or at least to restrict it, for the purpose of obtaining at least such contractual conditions as would raise them above the status of bare slaves.*

The immediate aim of the trade unions, therefore, was limited to waging the day-to-day struggle against Capital, as a means of defence against the continuous abuses of the latter, *i.e.,* questions concerning wages and working hours. This activity of the trade unions is not only justified, but also necessary. It is not advisable to dispense with it so long as the present system of production exists. On the contrary, it must become general by means of creating and uniting the trade unions in all countries.

On the other hand, *the trade unions, without being aware of it, became the focal points for the organisation of the working class,* just as the medieval municipalities and communities became such for the bourgeoisie. If trade unions have become indispensable for the guerilla fight between Capital and Labour, *they are even more important as organised bodies to promote the abolition of the very system of wage labour.*[1]

In this resolution a number of questions deserve special attention, particularly those concerning the *origin* and significance of the trade unions. Marx emphasises that the trade unions

[1] Resolution of the I.W.A. on Trade Unions, Geneva, 1866.

without being aware of it, became the focal points for the organisation of the working class, just as the medieval municipalities and communities became such for the bourgeoisie.

This comparison bears witness to the fact that Marx considered the trade unions not only "focal points" for the economic organisations; for the municipalities and communities in the Middle Ages were a weapon of the bourgeoisie in their struggle against feudalism, a weapon for the political struggle against the medieval system. Marx did not limit himself to this comparison, and already in this part of the resolution he says that the trade unions are *"even more important as organised means to promote the abolition of the very system of wage labour."* From this we see that Marx attached great political significance to the trade unions, that he regarded them least of all as neutral organisations, as non-political organisations. Every time that the trade unions closed themselves up in a narrow corporative framework, Marx would come out in sharp, lashing criticism of them.

This same Geneva Congress of the First International characterised the trade union movement of that period in the second part of that resolution, entitled *Their Present:*

The trade unions hitherto concentrated their attention too exclusively on the local and direct struggle against Capital. *They have not yet completely realised their power to attack the very system of wage slavery and present-day methods of production.* This is why they kept aloof from social and political movements. However, lately they are evidently *awakening and beginning to understand their great historical mission,* as can be seen, for example, from their participation in the recent political movement in England, from their higher conception of their functions in the United States and from the following resolution adopted at the enlarged conference of trade union delegates recently held at Sheffield:

"This Conference, fully approving of all the efforts made by the International Workingmen's Association to unite the workers of all countries into one fraternal union, urgently recommends the different societies whose representatives are present at the Conference to join the International, in the conviction that this is necessary for the progress and welfare of the whole working class." [1]

[1] *Ibid.*

In this part of the resolution we already see sharp criticism of all the trade unions that divorce themselves from politics, and here the significance of the trade unions that begin to understand their great historical mission is sharply emphasised.

If we consider the level of the trade union movement during the 'sixties, we shall realise the high plane on which Marx's appreciation of the trade union movement of his time stood. Marx, while understanding the extreme youth of the trade unions, did not consider it possible to make any kind of political concessions to them. He placed not only economic problems before them, but also general class tasks.

But Marx did not limit himself to defining the past and the present of the trade unions. In this resolution he says the following about their *future:*

> In addition to their original tasks, the trade unions must now learn how to act consciously as focal points for organising the working class in the greater interests of its complete emancipation. They must support every social and political movement directed towards this aim. By considering themselves champions and representatives of the whole working class, and acting accordingly, the trade unions must succeed in rallying round themselves all workers still outside their ranks. They must carefully safeguard the interests of the workers in the poorest-paid trades, as, for example, the farm labourers, who due to especially unfavourable circumstances have been deprived of their power of resistance. They must convince the whole world that their efforts are far from narrow and egoistic, but on the contrary, are directed towards the emancipation of the down-trodden masses.[1]

Here it is necessary to call attention to the fact that Marx again stresses the significance of the trade unions as *organising centres of the working class.* It is extremely important to note that the tasks set before the trade unions are: The struggle for the *complete* emancipation of the working class, the support of every social-political movement of the proletariat and the drawing of all workers into their ranks. Already in 1866 Marx emphasised the importance for the trade unions of defending the interests of the lower-paid workers, for example, the agricultural labourers.

[1] Resolution of the I.W.A. on Trade Unions, Geneva, 1866.

He expected the trade unions not to be "narrow and egoistic," that "their activities be directed towards emancipating the oppressed millions." This resolution was written sixty-nine years ago. But can it be said that it has now become antiquated, that these tasks are not the tasks of the trade unions in the capitalist countries to-day? By no means. Here, the basic tasks of the trade unions in the capitalist countries are mapped out with the clearness and concentration so characteristic of Marx. Nevertheless, Marx does not limit himself to this.

The question of the relationship between economics and politics was continuously before Marx and the First International, led by him, and he had to defend his point of view on this relationship against the Bakuninists, the adherents of Lassalle, and the trade unionists, etc. This is why he frequently came back to this question. In this connection his resolution adopted at the 1871 London Conference of the International Workingmen's Association is very characteristic and instructive. Here we read the following:

> In the presence of an unbridled reaction which violently crushes every effort at emancipation on the part of the working men, and pretends to maintain by brute force the distinction of classes and the political domination of the propertied classes resulting from it;
> considering that against this collective power of the propertied classes the working class cannot act, as a class, except by constituting itself into a political party, distinct from, and opposed to, all old parties formed by the propertied classes;
> that this constitution of the working class into a political party is indispensable in order to ensure the triumph of the social revolution and its ultimate end—the abolition of classes;
> that the combination of forces which the working class has already effected by its economical struggles ought at the same time to serve as a lever for its struggles against the political power of landlords and capitalists;
> the Conference recalls to the members of the *International*:
> That in the militant state of the working class, its economic movement and its political action are indissolubly united.[1]

[1] *Resolutions of the Conference of Delegates of the International Workingmen's Association, Assembled at London from 17th to 23rd September, 1871.* London, International Printing Office, 1871, p. 3. From the archives of the Marx-Engels-Lenin Institute, Moscow *Ed.*

This resolution, from the point of view of clarity and forceful-ness, is one of the classics in which the literary-political inheritance of Marx abounds. In this resolution the idea is again expressed that the trade unions must serve as a powerful lever in the hands of the working class for the struggle against the system of exploita-tion. To all the attempts of the Bakuninists to dissociate, to sep-arate economics from politics, to set off one against the other, the First International replies that *in the plan of struggle of the working class the economic movement and political activity are inseparably intertwined.*

Two months after this, in his letter to Bolte, Marx again raises the question of the relationship between politics and economics, and it is here that he defines the rôle of the economic struggle in the general class struggle of the proletariat. Marx writes:

The 'political movement' [1] of the working class naturally has as its final aim the conquest of 'political power' for it [the working class.—Ed.]; for this a 'previous organisation' of the working class, an organisation developed to a certain degree, is naturally necessary, which grows out of its economic forces themselves.

But on the other hand every movement in which the working class, as a class, opposes the ruling classes and seeks to compel them by 'pressure from without' is a *'political movement.'* For example, the attempt to obtain forcibly from individual capitalists a shortening of working hours in some individual factory or some individual trade by means of a strike, etc., is a purely economic movement. On the other hand a movement forcibly to obtain an eight-hour *law*, etc., is a political movement.

And in this way a *political* movement grows everywhere out of the individual economic movement of the workers, *i.e.*, a movement of the *class* to gain its ends in a general form, a form which possesses compelling force in a general social sense. If these movements presuppose a certain previous organisation, they in their turn are just as much means of developing the organisation.

Marx speaks of a "previous organisation of the working class," links up the purely economic movement with the political and the conditions for one movement developing into another,

---

[1] Words in quotation marks are in English in the original German text.

i.e., he sets forth precisely that which after his death was completely and intentionally forgotten and distorted by international reformism.

It was necessary not only to give an answer to the question of the significance of the economic struggle, but also on the mutual relationship between the economic and political organisations of the working class. The decision of the Hague Congress of the International Workingmen's Association (held September 2 to 7, 1872), is very characteristic in this regard. The Hague Congress, upon the proposal of Marx, adopted a resolution "on the political activity of the proletariat." In this resolution we read that in its struggle against the collective power of the possessing classes, the proletariat can take action, as a class, only after having organised its own political party as opposed to all the old parties founded by the possessing classes. Such organisation of the proletariat into a political party is necessary to ensure the victory of the social revolution and its ultimate aim—the abolition of classes.

> *The consolidation of the workers' forces attained in the economic struggle will also have to serve as a lever in the hands of this class for the struggle against the political power of its exploiters.* In view of the fact that the owners of the land and of capital always utilised their political privileges to guard and perpetuate their economic monopolies and to enslave labour, the conquest of political power comes to be the great task of the proletariat.[1]

After the Congress was closed Marx delivered a speech at a meeting, in which he emphasised the essence of the decisions that had been adopted. What then, in Marx's opinion, is most important in the decisions of the Hague Congress, which, as is well known, was the culminating point in the development of the First International?

The Hague Congress carried out some important work. It announced the necessity for the struggle of the working class both on the political and economic basis against the old disintegrating society.

We have to recognise that *in most Continental countries,* force

---

[1] Excerpt from James Guillaume, *Documents et Souvenirs (L'International).* My Italics.—*A.L.*

will have to be the lever of the revolution. *It is to force that in due time the workers will have to appeal if the dominion of labour is at long last to be established.*[1]

Again we see the *rôle* of the economic struggle in the general class struggle of the proletariat clearly and concisely defined. The trade unions must be "a lever" in the hands of the working class "for the struggle against the political power of its exploiters."

The question of the relationship between the economic and political struggle is the central question in the teachings of Marx. Therefore it is still less excusable for some of the Soviet historians to have taken such a thoughtless and slovenly attitude towards this question. Such a slovenly attitude was manifested by G. M. Stekloff in his book devoted to the First International. Comrade Stekloff writes that Marx in his commentary on the statutes of the International Workingmen's Association gave the following formulation: "The political struggle, as a means, is subordinated to the economic struggle of the proletariat." Furthermore, Comrade Stekloff tries to "justify" the author of this formulation, but he gets confused, for it would have been difficult to "justify" Marx had he actually written anything like this. Let us take Chapter III of this book of Comrade Stekloff, and here in the preamble set forth in full we read the following:

> *The economic emancipation of the working classes is, therefore, the great end to which every political movement ought to be subordinate as a means.*[2]

This is what Marx wrote. But are the *economic emancipation* of the working class and the *economic struggle* of the working class one and the same thing? If Marx had written what is ascribed to him by Comrade Stekloff, he would have been a vulgar Proudhonist, and we should have had to wage a struggle against him, for this would have meant the primacy of the economic struggle over the political. However, Marx, as we see, did not write anything of the kind. He wrote that the political movement must be wholly subordinated to the great aim of the economic emancipation of the proletariat. This formulation of

[1] I quote from G. M. Stekloff. *History of The First International,* p. 241. (Martin Lawrence, London; International Publishers, New York.)—*A.L.*

[2] *Ibid,* p. 49.

Marx's is irreproachable, for *political activity is not an aim, but a means for the achievement of the aim.* It is necessary determinedly to condemn such a thoughtless and politically harmful attitude towards the great teacher of international communism.

Karl Marx felt the pulse of the masses, he knew how to speak to them at every given moment. It will be very instructive in this connection to compare the *Communist Manifesto* (1847) and the *Inaugural Address* of the First International, written seventeen years later. The *Inaugural Address* of the First International is a document calling for the united front, aimed at rallying those strata and organisations of the working class which were not then ripe for communism. There is not even a word mentioned about communism in the whole of the *Inaugural Address,* but at the same time it is a *document communist to the core.* John Commons, an historian of the labour movement in the United States, wrote that the *"Inaugural Address* was a trade union document, not a Communist Manifesto."[1] Such an appraisal is doubly wrong, because it is not the form but the content that defines the character of the *Inaugural Address.* The *Inaugural Address* really raises as the major problems the economic conditions of the workers, labour legislation, etc., but in this document Marx also emphasises that *"the winning of political power has come to be the great duty of the working class,"* and then approaches the question of the Party, approaching it, however, in a special way. Here is what Marx wrote:

> One element of success they possess—numbers: but numbers weigh only in the balance if united by combination and led by knowledge. Past experience has shown how *disregard of that bond of brotherhood which ought to exist between the workmen of different countries and incite them to stand firmly by each other in all their struggles for emancipation, will be chastised by the common discomfiture of their incoherent efforts.*[2]

This is an unusual formulation for Marx. The working masses organised in the union are understood by Marx in a threefold manner: the masses organised in the trade union, the masses

---

[1] J. R. Commons, *History of Labour in the United States,* p. 205.

[2] G. M. Stekloff, *History of The First International,* p. 445. (Italics mine.—*A.L.*)

organised in the political party and the masses organised in the International. The formula about the leading *rôle* of *knowledge* is also unusual. What knowledge does he refer to? Is it to the leading *rôle* of university science? Is it to the leading *rôle* of the professors and academicians? By no means. Here *knowledge is the pseudonym of communism.* Marx intentionally used such words and formulations in order to penetrate more deeply into the midst of the masses:

> Its [the International Workingmen's Association—ED.] aim, wrote Engels, was to weld together into one huge army all the fighting forces of the working class of Europe and America. . . . The International was bound to have a programme which would not shut the door on the English trades' unions, the French, Belgian, Italian and Spanish Proudhonists and the German Lassalleans.[1]

> It was very difficult [writes Marx] to present the matter in such a way that our view might appear in a form acceptable to the present position taken by the labour movement. . . . . Time must elapse before the re-awakened movement will permit of the former boldness of language.[2]

Marx refers here to the form of exposing views, and not to their *essence*: when reference was made to the principle, to the essence of communist views, he was irreconcilable and unmerciful, but when it was a question of form, he manifested surpassing flexibility and ability to give the same content in various ways. This is what explains the "trade union language" of the *Inaugural Address,* the most remarkable document after the *Communist Manifesto.* This is how Marx, *with one and the same aim in view—to imbue the labour movement with communist consciousness*—changed forms and methods of approaching the masses, depending upon the level of the movement and the character of the working class organisations of the given period.

To define correctly the relationship between the economic and political struggle means to define correctly the relationship between the trade unions and the Party. While attaching

[1] Preface of Engels to the *Communist Manifesto.* Marx-Engels-Lenin Institute edition of the *Communist Manifesto,* Martin Lawrence, London; p. 44.

[2] Marx and Engels *Collected Works,* (German ed.) part iii, vol. 3, p. 199.

tremendous significance to the economic struggle of the proletariat and the trade unions, Marx always stressed the primacy of politics over economics, *i.e.*, stressed that which has been taken as a basis in the whole of the work of the Bolshevik Party and the Communist International.

When we speak about the primacy of politics over economics, it does not mean the turning of the trade unions into a political party or the adoption by the trade unions of a purely party programme, or the abolition of all differences between the trade unions and the party. No, this is not what Marx said. Marx emphasised the significance of the trade unions as organisational centres for the broad working masses, and fought against piling the party and the trade unions into one heap. He believed that the political and economic organisations of the proletariat have one and the same aim (the economic emancipation of the proletariat), but each applies its own specific methods in fighting for this aim. He understood primacy over economics in such a way that, in the first instance, he placed the political all-class tasks of the trade unions higher than the private corporative tasks, and secondly, that the political party of the proletariat must define the economic tasks and lead the trade union organisation itself.

CHAPTER II

Marx Against Proudhonism and Bakuninism

MARX forged his *Weltanschauung* (world-outlook) and his tactics in a bitter ideological-political struggle; he had to struggle primarily against the rather widespread theories of Proudhon. Proudhon was the type of petty-bourgeois socialist whose bold words were combined with reactionary theories. A talented publicist, a representative of sentimental deliquescent socialism, "from head to foot a philosopher, an economist of the petty bourgeoisie" (Marx), who upbraided the bourgeoisie with the glaring accusatory formula: "Ownership is theft." Proudhon considered himself a theoretician of the "working classes" and boldly began to come out with theoretical arguments on the philosophy of poverty. But theory seemed to be Proudhon's heel of Achilles because he could not go beyond the borders of the *bourgeois-liberal* science of his time, and this is what made Marx come out sharply against Proudhon and Proudhonism. Proudhon wrote a pretentious book, *The Philosophy of Poverty,* in which he wanted to establish laws for the development of society. In this book Proudhon made public the following thesis, which is rather of interest to us:

> Every upward movement in wages can have no other effect than that of a rise in wheat, in wine, etc., that is to say, the effect produced by a dearth. For what are wages? They are the cost price of wheat, etc., the integral price of everything. Let us go further still, wages are the proportion of the elements which compose wealth, and which are consumed reproductively each day by the mass of the workers. But to double wages is to bestow upon each of the producers a part greater than his product, which is contradictory; and if the rise only affects a small number of industries, the result is to provoke a general perturbation in exchange, in a word, a scarcity. It is impossible, I insist, for the strikes which result in an increase of wages not to lead to

a general dearness; that is as certain as that two and two make four.[1]

To these high-flown and asinine arguments of Proudhon Marx caustically adds: "We deny all these assertions, except that two and two is four."[2]

What is the political meaning of these theses of Proudhon? To keep the workers from fighting for higher wages. Since no amount of wage increases can do anything for the workers, since if wages are increased the price of foodstuffs is raised proportionately, the struggle of the workers is futile indeed.

Marx immediately grasped the essence of this reactionary philosophy and with the passion characteristic of him attacked the purely employers' arguments of this anarchist apostle. But Proudhon did not limit himself to this. He went further along this same path, determinedly coming out against the strike movement. Here is what we read in this *Philosophy of Poverty:*

> For workers the strike is illegal; and it is not only the penal code which says so, it is the economic system, it is the necessity of the established order. . . . That each workman should have the free disposal of his hand and of his person—that can be tolerated, but that workmen should undertake by combination to do violence to monopoly—that is what society can never permit.[3]

From this it is enough to see how great is the poverty of Proudhon's philosophy. Proudhon confused everything: the law of the formation of wages, the fixing of prices for commodities, the positive significance of association. He considered it impermissible for the workers to unite for the joint struggle against the employers, *i.e.,* he adhered to the viewpoint of the reactionary legislators of the capitalist countries of his time, who always punished the workers for forming associations. Marx knew with what he had to deal. He knew why such reactionary ideas were fashionable in France and therefore in his reply he analysed the

---

[1] Proudhon, *The Philosophy of Poverty.* Quoted by Marx in *Poverty of Philosophy,* Kerr edition, p. 181. [2] *Ibid.*
[3] *Ibid,* p. 185.

theoretical sterility of Proudhon and his political anti-labour conclusions. Here is what Marx wrote in the *Poverty of Philosophy* concerning this reactionary bosh of Proudhon:

> Big industry masses together in a single place a crowd of people unknown to each other. Competition divides their interests. But the maintenance of their wages, this common interest which they have against their employer, unites them in the same idea of resistance—combination. Thus, combination has always a double end, that of eliminating competition among themselves while enabling them to make a general competition against the capitalist. If the first object of resistance has been merely to maintain wages, in proportion as the capitalists in their turn have combined with the idea of repression, the combinations, at first isolated, have formed in groups, and, in face of constantly united capital, the maintenance of the association became more important and necessary for them than the maintenance of wages. This is so true that the English economists are all astonished at seeing the workers sacrifice a great part of their wages on behalf of the associations which, in the eyes of these economists, were only established in support of wages. In this struggle—a veritable civil war—*are united and developed all the elements necessary for a future battle. Once arrived at that point, association takes a political character.*[1]

Here Marx, with the clearness so peculiar to him, raised the question of the significance of the economic struggle of the proletariat (a real civil war!) and of bringing it to a higher level. But Marx did not limit himself to this. He analyses the various attitudes of the different scientific investigators towards the struggles of the bourgeoisie and the working class for their rights and interests. In reply to the purely employers' attitude of Proudhon towards the strike movement, Marx writes:

> Many researches have been made to trace the different historical phases through which the *bourgeoisie* has passed from the early commune to its constitution as a class.
> But when it becomes a question of rendering an account of the strikes, combinations, and other forms in which before our eyes the proletarians effect their organisation as a class,

[1] Marx, *The Povery of Philosophy*, p. 188 (Kerr edition). Italics mine.—*A.L.*

some are seized with fear while others express a transcendental disdain.

An oppressed class is the vital condition of every society based upon the antagonism of classes. The emancipation of the oppressed class therefore necessarily implies the creation of a new society. In order for the oppressed class to be emancipated it is necessary that the productive powers already acquired and the existing social relations should no longer be able to exist side by side. *Of all the instruments of production the greatest productive power is the revolutionary class itself.* The organisation of the revolutionary elements as a class supposes the existence of all the productive forces which can be engendered in the bosom of the old society.[1]

Marx at once noted that the bourgeois "impartial" scientists tried either to screen the economic struggle or to gloss it over. He bitterly criticises the negative attitude which the economic movement of the proletariat called forth among the bourgeois ideologists. Marx realised very well how the loud-mouthed "revolutionaries" of the type of Proudhon regard the struggle of the working class for its vital demands with "transcendental disdain." Have we not to-day such "revolutionaries" who express "transcendental disdain" for the economic struggle of the proletariat? Although there are few of them, yet we have some even in the midst of our own communist ranks.

What was the crux of all of Proudhon's misadventures? Engels, in his letter to Marx dated August 21, 1851, said the following on this subject:

I have read half of Proudhon, and I find your opinion fully confirmed. His appeal to the *bourgeoisie,* his harking back to Saint-Simon and a hundred other matters, even in the critical part, confirm that he looks upon the industrial class—the *bourgeoisie* and the proletariat—properly speaking as identical and as brought into opposition to each other only because the revolution has not been completed.[2]

In his letter to Kugelmann dated October 9, 1866, Marx writes about Proudhon:

[1] *Ibid,* p. 189. Italics mine.—*A.L.*
[2] Marx and Engels, *Letters,* published by "Moscow Worker," 1923, edited by V. Adoratsky.

Proudhon has done enormous mischief. His sham criticism and sham opposition to the utopians—(he himself is only a philistine utopian, whereas in the utopias of a Fourier, an Owen, etc., there is the presentiment and imaginative expression of a new world) attracted and corrupted the 'brilliant youth,' the students, and then the workmen, particularly those of Paris who, as workers in luxury trades, are strongly attached, without knowing it, to the old rubbish.[1]

In his letter to Engels of June 20, 1866, Marx deals with the "Proudhonised Stirner tendencies"; he says, "Proudhon aims at individualising humanity," and that from Proudhon's point of view:

> History in all other countries stops and the whole world waits until the French are sufficiently mature to bring about the social revolution.[2]

Proudhon, as is well known, is the founder of anarcho-syndicalism. Thus at any rate the anarcho-syndicalists speak and write, placing him higher than Marx, the defender of the State theory. But the anarcho-syndicalists conceal the fact that Proudhon was the enemy of the right of association and the strike movement. He hated strikes so deeply that he even *justified the murder of strikers*. Here is what Proudhon wrote in 1846 in the same *Philosophy of Poverty*:

> It is possible to agree to give every worker individually the liberty to dispose of himself and his hands as he pleases, but *society can under no circumstances permit* bands of workers, regardless of public interests and provisions of the law, to unite and violently to infringe upon the freedom and rights of the employers. To apply force against the employers and landowners, to disorganise the workshops, to stop work, to threaten capital really means *to conspire to cause general ruin*. For the authorities who shot down the miners in *Rive de Gier* it was a great misfortune. But here the authorities acted like ancient Brutus, who had to choose between fatherly love and his duty as consul; it was necessary to sacrifice his children in order to save the republic. Brutus did not hesitate and the generation that followed did not dare to condemn him for it.[3]

[1] Marx, *Letters to Kugelmann*, Martin Lawrence, London.
[2] Marx and Engels, *Letters*, edited by Adoratsky, Moscow, 1933.
[3] P. F. Proudhon, *Systeme des Contradictions économiques*, Vol. I.

One might have expected Proudhon later on to give up this viewpoint, which was that of an industrialist, but no, he persisted in it to his grave. In his book, *On the Political Capacity of the Working Classes,* completed in 1865 (the year of his death), Proudhon quoted this excerpt from his *Philosophy of Poverty* and further develops his idea.[1] In this book Proudhon sharply attacked the government of Napoleon III, especially the leader of the Liberals of his time, Marcel Olivier, who argued for the right of association for workers, on the ground that what is not forbidden to some cannot and must not be forbidden to the many. Proudhon failed to realise here also that the bourgeoisie declares itself for the right of association not because of its own desires, but because it is compelled to do so under the pressure of the continual struggle of the workers. Proudhon attacks the supporters of the right of association and writes:

> The law permitting association is, as a matter of fact, anti-juridical and anti-economic, contradicting every social régime and public order. Any concession made in connection with this law is an abuse and is null and void in itself—it is cause for making public charges and instituting criminal proceedings. . . .
> I especially object to the new law: association for the purpose of increasing or lowering wages is absolutely the same as association for the purpose of increasing or lowering prices of foodstuffs or other commodities.[2]

What can one say about these arguments? In such a fashion only a frenzied petty-bourgeois can argue; one who, on the one hand, shouts " 'Property is robbery!' and, on the other, 'Shoot down the strikers!' "

How do Proudhon's supporters reconcile these slogans? One of them, Maxim Leroix, who wrote the preface to the book *De la Capacitié Politique des Classes Ouvrières,* in his effort to extol the greatness of Proudhon, gives a number of quotations from Proudhon on the class struggle, on the war between Labour and Capital, and sums up the essence of Proudhonism in the following way:

[1] P. F. Proudhon, *De la Capacité Politique des Classes Ouvrières,* p. 380.
[2] P. F. Proudhon, *Ibid.,* p. 388.

The class struggle—but at the same time no call for social destruction. The class struggle—but at the same time a call to the workers to collaborate with the middle classes. The class struggle —and at the same time, prohibition of strikes. . . . The class struggle—but at the same time class collaboration. . . .[1]

How does Leroix himself solve these striking contradictions of Proudhon? He does not solve them, nor does he explain them; he claims that the crux of the teachings of Proudhon lies in mutualism, that

Proudhon did not propose either the mysticism of an emancipation catastrophe, nor a programme of war strategy, because he never imagined the working class as a class, as toilers without a master, toilers who do not know any dogmas, who crave for truth in the process of eternal becoming, as a class which executes the experiment of Saint Simon on a large scale.[2]

The conclusion of these rather vague arguments is: Proudhon "was a deeper thinker than Marx."

If the anarcho-syndicalists prefer to have Proudhon, the enemy of strikes and the class struggle, as their teacher that is their business. As far as we are concerned, we prefer to have Marx as our spiritual teacher, Marx who defended strikes and the right of association, who all his life taught the working class how to fight the bourgeoisie, how to unite the struggle for the workers' immediate demands with the struggle for their final goal.

Could Marx and Engels to any degree subscribe to the unprecedented confusion that Proudhon brought into the labour movement? Of course not. They quite naturally waged a bitter struggle against Proudhon and his theories.

But the Proudhonists, who at first came out against trade unions, against the right to strike, etc., were later compelled under life's hard blows to change their point of view. Marx, in his letter to Engels, dated September 12, 1868, writes:

The fact that the Proudhonist *braves Belges* (fine Belgians) and Frenchmen, who dogmatically held forth in Geneva (in 1866) and

---

[1] P. F. Proudhon, *De la Capacité Politique des Classes Ouvrières*, pp. 22-30.
[2] *Ibid.*, p. 30.

in Lausanne (1867) against the trade unions, etc., are to-day their most fanatical adherents, denotes great progress.[1]

From this letter we can see that the Proudhonists turned the theory of their teacher inside out, but this did not in any way improve his theory. Precisely for this reason Marx and Engels waged a determined struggle against the theory and practice of the Proudhonists.

The greatest of his adherents, Michael Bakunin, continued Proudhon's course. Bakunin realised the weaknesses and short-comings in the world-outlook of Proudhon. Bakunin, who highly valued Proudhon, characterised him in the following way:

> Proudhon, despite all his efforts to be a realist, has remained an idealist and metaphysician. Proudhon, despite all his efforts to shake the traditions of classic idealism, has remained an incorrigible idealist, who was inspired now by the Bible, now by Roman Law, and remained a metaphysician to the very end, as I told him two months before his death.[2]

It is difficult to give a more destructive characterisation of one's "teacher," as Bakunin himself often called Proudhon. It is not surprising, then, that Marx carried on a merciless struggle against the idealistic metaphysical confusion of Proudhon.

In comparison with Proudhon, Bakunin was doubtlessly an ace. Bakunin was a great revolutionary figure, a rebel, who, as Hertzen said, was always to be found "at the extreme end," a man with tremendous energy and great organisational talent. But he was a nobleman in rebellion. His world-outlook represented a mixture of Hegel, Stirner and the Russian Pugachev movement. He did not see classes, he always referred to the people. Bakunin did not speak of the working class, he wrote more about "the labourers," "the poor people," "the poverty-stricken sections of the population," "the common labouring man," and contrasted the revolutionary spirit of the *lumpen proletariat* with the reactionary spirit of the labour aristocracy, among whom he included large sections of the workers. Bakunin did not approve of Marx organising circles, giving lectures to

[1] Marx and Engels, *Collected Works.*
[2] W. Polonsky, *M. A. Bakunin* (Russian edition), Vol. I, p. 171.

c

workers, etc. In his letter to Annenkov, dated December 28, 1847, he writes that Marx occupies himself with the same idle work as formerly; he spoils the workers by turning them into reasoners.[1]

What, then, did Bakuninism represent, as a system? Bakunin himself called his system *"the anarchist system of Proudhon extended by us, developed and freed by us of all metaphysical, idealistic and doctrinaire frills."*[2]

Thus, we have before us a more perfected Proudhonism, which also was just as far from Marxism theoretically and politically as the pure Proudhonism.

Bakunin denied every state, political struggle or political organisation of the proletariat. The struggle between Marx and Bakunin was a struggle between two different world-outlooks, two different systems and theories; it was a struggle between two different political and tactical lines, which of course could not but be reflected in the organisational question. Thus, the organisational problem was not the cause but the occasion for the split.

What *rôle* did the trade unions and the economic struggle play in Bakunin's theories? In his pamphlet, *Policy of the International,* Bakunin writes:

> The emancipation of the workers is the cause of the workers themselves, which is emphasised in the introduction to our general statutes. This is a thousand times correct. This is the chief basis of our great union. However, the workers in most cases are ignorant, they still do not know theory. Consequently, *they have only one path left, the path of practical emancipation.* And what should and must this practice be? It can be only one: the struggle based on the solidarity of the workers against the bosses; that is trade unions, organisations, and federations of resistance fund societies.
>
> Convinced of this truth, we raise the question: "What policy should the International adhere to during this more or less lengthy period of time separating us from that terrible social revolution which we now foresee?"
>
> Rejecting, in accordance with its statutes, all politics on a local as well as a national scale, *the International will impart to the workers' agitational activities in all countries an exclusively economic character,* setting the goal: shorten working hours and

[1] W. Polonsky, *M. A. Bakunin* (Russian edition), Vol. I, p. 171.
[2] *Ibid.,* p. 138.

increase wages, using as a means the consolidation of the working masses and the organised collection of resistance funds.[1]

Here we see that Bakunin refers to *"purely economic agitation."* He speaks about the creation of resistance fund societies for the *purely economic struggle,* says that the workers are ignorant and therefore must not occupy themselves with too difficult problems, etc. The most that Bakunin permits is a federation of resistance fund societies. This shows that although Bakunin went further than Proudhon, he yet remained on one and the same path with him. He did not realise that the trade unions are centres for organising the masses, that they are the ones which prepare the masses for the struggle for the dictatorship of the proletariat; he failed to see just what Marx saw in the very first steps of the trade unions.

It is interesting to note the views of Bakunin on what the workers must *demand.* In the draft programme of the International Revolutionary Society, Bakunin writes:

> The worker demands and must demand: (1) Equality—political, economic and social—for all classes and all peoples on earth; (2) the abolition of inherited property; (3) transfer of the land to the agricultural associations for use by them, and the transfer of capital and all means of production to the workers' industrial associations.[2]

Whereas Marx raised the question of the *abolition* of classes, Bakunin speaks of the *equality* of classes. (True, later on, under the pressure of Marx's criticism, Bakunin abandoned this formulation.) Bakunin already here expressed the idea of transferring the enterprises to the workers' industrial associations, the idea that was afterwards taken as a basis for all the theories developed by the French, Spanish and Italian anarchists and anarcho-syndicalists. It is a theory that never has been or could have been realised in practice anywhere, although the anarchists, opposed to power, succeeded in establishing their power over considerable territories (for example, Machno in Russia).

[1] Bakunin, *Policy of the International* (Russian edition). Italics mine.—*A.L.*
[2] *Miscellany—M. Bakunin—Unpublished Materials and Articles.* (Russian edition). Published by Politkatorzhan (Political Prisoners) Society, 1926.

What was the attitude of Marx and Engels towards these theories? The whole conception of Marx on the *rôle* of the trade unions, the relations between economics and politics, impelled him to wage a determined struggle against these petty-bourgeois theories. Although Bakunin said a great deal about the economic struggle and about "only economic demands," he saw in the trade unions an amalgamation of ignorant people. He believed that the masses were in need of a hero who could lead them to the promised land of anarchism. Bakunin on the one hand depended upon a hero, and, on the other hand, on the spontaneous merciless revolt of the ignorant masses. Marx depended upon the masses, the class, upon organisation. This is why, during the period of the First International, Bakuninism and Marxism clashed so sharply. How deep was the gulf between Bakuninism and Marxism in questions of principle may be seen from the fact that even to-day we are still compelled to carry on the struggle against vestiges of Bakuninism in a number of the Latin-European and Latin-American countries.

CHAPTER III

The Struggle against Lassalleanism and all other forms of German Opportunism

MARX attentively observed the development of the labour movement in Germany. The revolution of 1848 was the highest peak in the activity of the labour movement in Germany during that period. After 1848 the wave began to subside, the labour movement was split, considerable sections of the revolutionary elements had to emigrate to France, England and America. In Germany itself all sorts of fraternal organisations, mutual aid societies and other trade unions in embryo began to spring up.

Marx and Engels maintained close contact both with the revolutionary working-class emigrants and with the revolutionary elements within the country. After 1848 a period of political and ideological reaction set in in Germany and a number of Marx's companions-in-arms left the revolutionary movement. Marx at that time energetically worked on putting the finishing touches to his philosophic world-outlook, on working out his economic system, simultaneously carrying on vast literary-political activities. Towards the end of the 'fifties the repressions grew less severe. The labour movement in Germany revived. Lassalle organised the General Workmen's Union (1863), and sharply raised the question of the political tasks and rights of the working class. Lassalle, who came forward at the moment when this animation began, responded to the change in the mood of the working masses and this is why the General Workmen's Union came to be very popular. Marx and Engels valued Lassalle: "Lassalle, in spite of all his 'buts,' is firm and energetic," Marx wrote to Engels on March 10, 1853.[1] "Lassalle is the only one who still dares to correspond with London, and we must see that he does not tire of it," Marx wrote to Engels on July 18, 1853.[2] In his letter to

[1] Marx and Engels, *Collected Works*, German ed., part III, Vol. I, pp. 456-57.　　　　　　　　　　　*Ibid.*, p. 491.

Schweitzer, dated October 13, 1868, Marx writes: "After fifteen years of slumber, Lassalle has roused again the labour movement in Germany. This will remain his undying merit." [1]

However, from the very outset Marx and Engels saw a number of serious defects in his theory and practice. The differences grew as Lassalle kept on revealing his incorrect line. Lassalle looked with distrust upon the workers' struggle for the right of association and did not see any good in strikes.

"Association rights cannot be of any use to the worker. They cannot bring about a serious improvement in the workers' conditions."

Such are the arguments of Lassalle. Lassalle spoke about the "sad experiences" acquired by the British strikers. He considered the struggle for higher wages to be hopeless, for the working class *cannot change the iron law of wages,* which, according to him, *was the corner-stone of all economic perception.* As a panacea for all troubles Lassalle put up two demands: general suffrage and State subsidies to producers' associations. He therefore rejected the economic struggle of the working class and denied the usefulness of the trade unions.

This whole conception of Lassalle's was alien to Marx.

"Lassalle was against the movement to organise unions," Marx writes to Engels in his letter of February 13, 1865. "Liebknecht organised unions amongst the Berlin printers against the wishes of Lassalle."

Such a view of Lassalle on the trade unions and on industrial association could not but call forth severe criticism from Marx and Engels, who saw immediately that the General Workmen's Union was a peculiar petty-bourgeois party of a profoundly sectarian character.

The strife between Marx and Lassalle began in connection with the so-called iron law of wages. This iron law of wages as a matter of fact was merely a repetition of the Proudhonist theories and the Malthusian law of population. What is the essence of this theory? That no matter what the worker does, no matter how hard he fights, he will not be able to improve his condition. This theory of the rejection and futility of organised economic struggles

---

[1] Marx and Engels, *Selected Letters,* published by Marx-Engels-Lenin Institute.

could not meet with sympathy on the part of Marx.   Marx sharply criticised the iron law of wages by proving that wages consist of two parts.   They include a physical and a social minimum; the latter changes with the socio-historical conditions. Lassalle not only insisted upon his iron law of wages, but turned more and more towards government subsidies.

> I have repeatedly emphasised that I want individual, voluntary associations, but these, in order to come into existence, must receive the necessary capital by a grant of State credits.[1]

> In order to emancipate your class, in order to emancipate not only a few individual workers, but labour itself, millions and millions of thalers are required, and these can be granted only by the State and by legislation.[2]

This is how simply Lassalle solved the labour problem.   At first we must fight for general suffrage; "the government will give many millions of thalers."   Could Marx fail to come out against this harmful and utterly petty-bourgeois utopia?
On April 9, 1863, Marx wrote to Engels:

> Itzig . . . [Lassalle.—A. L.] the day before yesterday sent me his open letter to the Central Workers' Committee for the Leipzig Workers' (read old type workers') Congress.   He conducts himself quite like the future dictator of the workers, pretentiously casting about phrases he has borrowed from us.   The dispute between wages and capital he settles 'playfully, easily' (verbatim).   Namely, the workers must agitate for *general suffrage* and then send to the Chamber of Deputies people of his type, "armed with the bare weapon of science."   Then they will organise workers' factories, the capital for which the State will advance, and these institutions will by and by embrace the entire country.   At all events this is surprisingly new.[3]

This is how Marx came out against Lassalle; first of all, because Lassalle adhered to a *wrong programme;* secondly, because Lassalle adhered to *wrong tactics;* and thirdly, because he had a *wrongly built organisation.*

[1] Lassalle, speech made on April 16, 1863.
[2] F. Lassalle, Vol. IV, *Appeal of the General Workers' Union of Germany to the Workers of Berlin,* p. 51.
[3] Marx and Engels, *Collected Works* (German ed.), Part III, Vol. 3, p. 136.

Schweitzer, who after the death of Lassalle became President of the General Workers' Union of Germany, began to sponsor the right of association and even greet the struggle for wages. However, although Schweitzer turned away from his teacher, yet he comes to the following conclusions in a whole series of his articles:

1. A strike out of necessity is a failure from the economic viewpoint.
2. Nevertheless the strike is an excellent means of causing the labour movement to erupt and of raising it to the altitude at which the working class is sufficiently mature for its proper class perception.
3. Where the labour movement can come out openly for its ultimate aim, strikes, as a rule, should not be sanctioned, because the working class needs its full strength to attain its final aim—change of the social bases—whereas strikes divert the strength of many from the one common aim, without achieving the supposed gain—a rise in wages.[1]

We see that the world-outlook of Schweitzer is not so straightforward as that of Lassalle. New notes can be heard in his arguments—he is both *for and against*. In 1868 Schweitzer took the initiative in convening a national workers' congress in Germany "for the purpose of pushing the movement ahead by means of a stoppage of work." This congress aimed at consolidating the already existing trade unions and at organising new ones; the newly organised trade unions struck against the organisational and general principles of Lassalleanism.

Marx closely and attentively followed the evolution of the General Workers' Union of Germany, for he knew that confusion reigned among the adherents of Lassalle, especially with regard to the question of the right of association. In his letter dated February 18, 1865, Marx wrote to Engels as follows:

Associations, with the trade unions arising from them, are not only extremely important as means for organising the working class for the struggle against the *bourgeoisie*—the importance of this means is seen in the fact that even the workers of the United States, in spite of the existence there of suffrage and of a republic,

[1] J. B. von Schweitzer: *Die Gewerkschaftsfrage (The Trade Union Question)* (German ed.) Weltgeist Bücher, Berlin, pp. 38-39.

cannot get along without them—but we see that in Prussia and in Germany the right of association is besides a breach in the domination of the police and bureaucracy; it tears asunder the 'Farmhands' Law and the economy of the nobility in the village; in brief, it is a measure for granting subjects their majority, which measure the progressive party, any *bourgeois* party in the opposition in Prussia, if it is not insane, could sooner grant a hundred times than the Prussian government, especially the government of a Bismarck.[1]

In the same letter Marx dwells on the famous Lassallean idea of government subsidies. Here is what Marx writes about this "Royal Prussian Government Subsidising of Co-operative Societies. . . ."

> Beyond a doubt the disappointment in Lassalle's hapless illusion concerning socialist intervention on the part of a Prussian government will come. The logic of things will have its say. But the *honour* of the workers' party demands that it reject these optical illusions even before their flimsy texture is rent by experience. *The working class is revolutionary or it is nothing.*[2]

This fine letter to Engels sheds light upon the hostility felt by Marx for Lassalle's principles. *The working class is revolutionary or nothing.* This is what defines the line of action of Karl Marx.

Marx considered the General Workers' Union to be a sectarian organisation and repeatedly returned to this question. This viewpoint about the sectarian nature of the General Workers' Union Marx constantly expressed in his letter to Schweitzer. He gives a classic definition of just what sectarianism is. Here is what Marx writes in his letter to Schweitzer of October 13, 1868:

> Just because he is the founder of a sect he [Lassalle] denied all natural connection with the former labour movement in Germany. He made the same mistake as Proudhon, of seeking the genuine basis for his agitation not among the real elements of the class movement, but of wanting to prescribe to the latter its course according to a certain doctrinaire recipe.
>
> You yourself have experienced the contrast between a sectarian movement and a class movement. The sect views its *raison d'être* [reason for its existence] and its *point d'honneur* [point of honour], not in what it has *in common* with the class movement, but in a

---

[1] Marx and Engels, *Collected Works*, (German ed.) Part III, Vol. 3, p. 240.
[2] *Ibid.*, p. 240.

special shibboleth that distinguishes it from this movement. But when you proposed to convene a congress in Hamburg for founding trade unions, you were able to defeat sectarian resistance only by the threat to resign from the honourable post of president. Furthermore, you were compelled to assume a dual personality, to declare that at one time you had acted as head of a sect, while at another as an organ of the class movement.

The dissolution of the General Workers' Union of Germany gave you the impetus to make a considerable step forward and declare, prove, if you like, that now a new period of development had arrived, and that the sectarian movement was now ripe enough to merge in the class movement, and put an end to all 'isms'. . . . As far as the true content of the sect was concerned, it (the sect) would introduce it (the content) into the general movement as an element of enrichment like all former workers' sects. Instead of this, you in fact demanded that the class movement subordinate itself to a special sectarian movement. Your non-friends have drawn the conclusions from this that you desire at all cost to preserve "your own labour movement." [1]

When just before the Hamburg Congress Schweitzer sent to Marx the draft statutes of his new General Workers' Union, Marx utilised this occasion to severely criticise the draft. Marx considered a political trade union federation unreal, and bureaucratic centralisation extremely dangerous, especially for Germany.

In his letter to Schweitzer dated September 13, 1868, Marx wrote:

As for the draft of the constitution, I consider it a failure on questions of principle, and I believe I have as much experience in trade unionism as any contemporary. Without going into details at this point, I will merely say that the organisation, while ever so suitable for secret societies and sectarian movements, contradicts the nature of trade unionism. If it [the organisation.—Ed.] were possible—I declare *tout bonnement* (quite frankly) that it is impossible—it would not be desirable, least of all in Germany. Here, where the workers are under the thumb of bureaucracy from childhood on and believe in authority, in the constituted authorities, it is a foremost task to teach them how to walk by themselves.

[1] Marx and Engels, *Letters.* Edited by Adoratsky, published 1932. (Russian edition.)

Your plan is also impractical in other respects. In your union you have three independent powers of different origin: (1) The committee elected by the trades; (2) the president, a wholly super-fluous personage elected by general vote; (3) the congress, elected by the locals. Thus there are clashes everywhere and this is supposed to promote rapid action. Lassalle made a serious mistake when he borrowed the *élu du suffrage universal* (person elected by universal suffrage) from the French Constitution of 1852. And in a trade union movement at that. The latter hinges largely on money questions and you will soon discover that here all dictatorship ceases.[1]

This letter calls attention not only to the businesslike destructive criticism of Lassalle-Schweitzer super-centralism, but also to the formulation as a principle of the question of the necessity of teaching the German workers to "walk by themselves." This problem was frequently dealt with in the letters of Marx and Engels. They knew what bureaucratic drill-sergeant methods were, and feared that if the Party and trade union organisations were built in a bureaucratic manner, it could bring endless harm to the working class of Germany. On this question, just as on all others, Marx proved to be prophetically right. The bureaucratic centralism of German Social-Democracy, which re-echoed the "national" traditions of the Prussian barrack square, has been a damper on the labour movement of Germany to this very day.

Marx and Engels time and again came out against the dictatorial methods of Schweitzer, the successor of Lassalle. They proved that his line could not but cause his organisation to fall apart and that it was necessary to choose between a mass trade union organisation and a narrow, sectarian, semi-political, semi-trade union organisation.

After the Hamburg Congress on September 26, 1868, Marx wrote to Engels:

One of the ridiculous operations of Schweitzer—he was doubt-less compelled to act so by the prejudices of his army and as president of the General Workers' Union of Germany—is that he was compelled to swear constantly *in verbis magistri* (in the language of a master) and at every concession to the demands of the real labour movement, to argue apprehensively that it (this

[1] Letter of Marx to Schweitzer, dated Sept. 13, 1868. (August Bebel: *From My Life*, published 1914, pp. 215-16.)

movement) does *not* contradict the dogmas of the sole redeeming Lassallean confession of faith. The Hamburg Congress quite correctly felt instinctively that the General Workers' Union of Germany, as a specific organisation of the Lassallean sect, would be jeopardised by the real labour movement through trade unions, etc.[1]

The sectarian character of the Lassalle organisation was incompatible with the growth of the movement. Marx emphasised time and again that it was impossible to jam the broad masses into a sectarian organisation.

Marx expressed his opinion on this subject in his letter to Bolte, dated November 23, 1871:

. . . The Lassalle organisation is merely a sectarian organisation, and as such is hostile to the organisation of the real labour movement, inspired by the International.[2]

The question of the attitude towards the Lassalle theories was again raised by Marx and Engels in connection with the unity congress between the Lassalleans and Eisenachers, held in 1875 in Gotha.

Marx analysed the draft programme with merciless severity, and here he for the first time came out in the Press stating his attitude towards the Lassallean principles. Concerning the proposed "iron law," Marx wrote that, as is well known, in this law only the word iron belonged to Lassalle, which he borrowed from Goethe; that "*Lassalle did not know* (emphasis by Marx) what wages were and that, following the bourgeois economists, he mistook appearance for reality"; that "Lassalle imagines that *it is just as easy to build a new society with State loans as it is to build a new railroad.*" [3]

In his letter to Bebel, dated March 18-28, 1875, Engels writes the following about the Gotha programme:

. . . Nothing is said about *the organisation of the working class as a class, by means of trade unions.* This is a very important point, because these, as a matter of fact, are the real class organisations of the proletariat, in which the latter wages its day-to-day

---

[1] Marx and Engels, *Collected Works* (German ed.), Part II, Vol. 4, p. 102.
[2] Marx and Engels, *Selected Letters* (Russian ed.), p. 259. Edited by Adoratsky, Moscow, 1928.
[3] Marx-Engels, *Critiques*, pp. 33-35. Berlin, 1918.

struggle against Capital; in which it schools itself, and which even to-day, under the most ruthless reaction (as now in Paris), simply can no longer be knocked to pieces. Considering the importance which these organisations attain also in Germany, it would in our opinion be absolutely necessary to make mention of them in the programme and if possible to reserve a place for them in the organisation of the party.[1]

Liebknecht and Bebel were extremely dissatisfied with the sharp criticism made by Marx and Engels concerning the Gotha programme. Bebel, in his memoirs, after quoting this letter of Engels, adds melancholically:

> It was no easy job to come to an agreement with the two old fellows in London. What we considered prudent calculation and skilful tactics they considered weakness and irresponsible complaisance.[2]

This remark is, indeed, very characteristic of Bebel. In German Social-Democracy, from the first days it was founded, the habit gained foothold of explaining their retreat from Marxist principles by referring to "tactics," as if tactics were a thing separate and apart from principles.

Marx and Engels were against amalgamating the adherents of Lassalle with the Eisenachers, inasmuch as the platform for this unification was not only ambiguous, but also incorrect. Marx expressed this in his letter to Bracke dated May 5, 1875:

> *Every step of actual movement is more important than a dozen programmes.* If it was thus not possible—and contemporary circumstances do not permit this—to go beyond the Eisenach programme, then there should have been concluded an *agreement for action* against the common enemy. But if a programme of principles is drawn up (instead of postponing this until it has been prepared for by prolonged joint activity), a landmark is erected before the whole world by which it can measure the extent of the party movement.[3]

Thus we see where Marx stood when the trade union movement of Germany was still in its infancy. He followed up every

---

[1] Engels to Bebel, *Selected Letters* (German ed.), p. 275, Berlin, 1918.
[2] August Bebel, *From My Life*, Vol. 2, p. 338, Stuttgart, 1914.
[3] Marx, Letter to W. Bracke (May 5, 1875) accompanying *Critique of the Gotha Programme*, p. 62. (Martin Lawrence, London; International Publishers, New York.)

step of the labour movement, coming out openly and in letters on the political and tactical lines, incidentally correcting mistakes, emphasising the weak and strong sides of the movement.

In the labour movement of Germany at that time we had not only the Lassalle-Schweitzer efforts to destroy the trade unions by attempts to turn them into a party, but the reverse tendencies were also observed, *i.e.*, a recognition of the trade union as the only form of the labour movement. Here it was Johann Philipp Becker, leader of the German Section of the International Workingmen's Association, who erred.

During the period when a political party of the proletariat began to be formed in Germany, the most difficult and complicated problem was that of the mutual relations between the different workers' educational societies of all shades, the trade unions and the party. We saw above how Lassalle and Schweitzer solved this problem and how Marx and Engels objected to such a type of organisation. Johann Philipp Becker, in connection with the formation of a political labour party (Eisenachers), in 1869 submitted a draft proposal in which he stated that the trade unions were the only true form of the labour movement. Becker formulated his proposal as follows:

In view of the fact that the trade unions alone afford the correct form of workers' unions and of future society in general, and in view of the fact that the technical knowledge predominating in their ranks facilitates the creation of a firm base for exact social science:

. . . that in proportion as the organisation of the trade union is being completed, the condition for the further existence of the mixed unions (as, for example, the General Workers' Union of Germany and the Workers' Educational Society) ceases to operate, having performed their mission as initiators.[1]

Only as a result of the failure to understand clearly what a party is and how it must be built was it possible to raise the question in such a light. Bebel was very much excited about this proposal and inquired from Marx how he regarded the draft. Marx replied that he had had nothing to do with this draft.

Engels at once sharply reacted to this, expressing not only his own but also Marx's viewpoint on the subject:

[1] *Vorbote, Geneva* 1869, p. 103.

Old man Becker has evidently gone out of his mind altogether. How can he decree that the trade unions are to be the genuine workers' associations and the basis of all organisation, that the other societies are to exist alongside only temporarily, etc. All of this, mind you, in a country where proper trade unions do not even exist yet. And what a confused 'organisation.' On the one hand each trade becomes centralised in a national supreme body, and on the other hand, the different trades of each locality become centralised in turn in a local supreme body. If discord is to reign for ever, this arrangement should be introduced. But *au fond* (at bottom) he is no better than the old German itinerant journeyman who wants to save his 'sleeping-quarters' in every city and mistakes these 'sleeping-quarters' for the unity of the workers' organisation.[1]

Marx could not be lured by mere revolutionary phrases. Just as soon as some of the then modern socialists would begin to make too much noise, he would determinedly come out against them. In this connection the different attitudes of Marx and of Bernstein towards Most are very characteristic. Bernstein accused Most of Leftism, but simultaneously, under cover of this, he tried to spread his Right-wing, petty-bourgeois ideas. To these smuggling attempts of Bernstein Marx instantly reacted. In his letter to Sorge dated September 19, 1879, he wrote:

Our points of dispute with Most are by no means those of the Zürich gentlemen (the trio consisting of Dr. Höchberg, Bernstein, his secretary, and C. H. Schramm). Our reproach to Most is not that his 'liberty' is too revolutionary, but that it has *no revolutionary content, but only spins revolutionary phrases.*

Exactly: the struggle of revolutionary Marxism against "Left" phrases has nothing in common with the struggle of the reformists of all shades and colours against the "Lefts." In this we see the strict line of principle maintained by Marx and Engels in their struggle for the party tactics.

Marx and Engels waged a merciless struggle against all forms of opportunism, unscrupulousness and "family relationship" in politics. They never could tolerate the glossing over of theoretical or political differences and were always, according to the

[1] Marx and Engels, *Collected Works* (German ed.), Part III, Vol. 4, p. 214.

expression of Gleb Uspensky, "ready to take up the fight." This trait of theirs was particulary emphasised by Lenin in 1907, in his preface to the *Letters of Marx and Engels to Sorge*. In view of the fact that they stood nearest to the labour movement of Germany, their leading *rôle* in the struggle for theoretical clearness, political consistency and tactical boldness is seen here more distinctly.

Marx and Engels were the first to give the alarm about alien elements penetrating the ranks of German Social-Democracy, and demanded strict control over "this pack of Ph.D's, students, etc., and professorial socialist rabble," who already then played a disproportionately big *rôle* in the ranks of German Social-Democracy. Marx protested against "those fellows, nonentities theoretically, good-for-nothing practically, who want to pull the teeth of the socialism which they have brewed for themselves according to university recipes, particularly the teeth of the Social-Democratic Party; they want to enlighten the workers, or, as they say, provide them with 'elements of education' through their muddled half-baked knowledge. They are poor, counter-revolutionary windbags. Well."[1]

Can we say that this characterisation of "scientific" socialists has now gone out of date? No, such counter-revolutionary windbags are to-day hiding behind the socialist and even Marxist banner; thousands upon thousands of them are in the ranks of the Second International.

Marx and Engels fought against all forms of sectarianism and opportunism and especially against the establishment of incorrect relationships between the Party and the trade unions. The letters of Marx and Engels to Liebknecht, Bebel, Kautsky, etc., are a fine example of party-political vigilance and consistency of principle. Every time that the Party or trade union organisation made some mistake, Marx and Engels sounded the alarm, emphasising that such mistakes threatened to distort the general line. This is why it is of tremendous importance to study the principles governing the line of Marx and Engels on all problems in controversy with the Lassalle and Eisenach organisations and the leaders of the German-Democratic Party.

[1] Letter of Marx to Sorge, Sept. 19, 1879.

CHAPTER IV

Marx and the Trade Union Movement in England

THE first half of the nineteenth century was characterised by rapid growth and development in the trade union movement in England. Immediately after the repeal, in 1824, of the law prohibiting labour associations, the trade unions emerged from underground and began to spread all over England. The British trade unions were narrow craft organisations and had only practical aims (shortening of the working day, increases in wages, etc.). Marx and Engels observed the development of the British labour movement during the course of many years. The first serious book of Engels was devoted to the condition of the working class in England; that brilliant work of Marx known as *Capital,* is built on an analysis of British economics and the British labour movement. Both Marx and Engels attached much significance to the British trade unions precisely because they waged a merciless struggle for improving the conditions of the workers, considering that "the condition of the working class is the real basis and starting point for all social movements to-day" (Engels).

Marx and Engels saw the narrow craft character of the trade unions, saw their narrow outlook, and yet they considered the trade unions a serious step forward along the road of development of the British, and not only the British, labour movement.

> Something more is needed [Engels wrote] than Trade Unions and strikes to break the power of the ruling class. But what gives these unions and the strikes arising from them their real importance is this, that they are the first attempt of the workers to abolish competition. They imply the recognition of the fact that the supremacy of the *bourgeoisie* is based wholly upon the competition of the workers among themselves, *i.e.,* upon their want of cohesion. And precisely because the unions direct themselves against the vital nerve centre of the present social order, however

49

one-sidedly, in however narrow a way, are they so dangerous to this social order. The working men cannot attack the *bourgeoisie,* and with it, the whole existing order of society, at any sorer point than this.[1]

The main trouble of the British trade union movement of that period was the confused socialist outlook even of the most advanced leaders of that time. British socialism then was extremely lean and anæmic. Here is how Engels characterises the socialists of that period:

> English socialism arose with Owen, a manufacturer, and proceeds therefore with great consideration towards the bourgeoisie and great injustice towards the proletariat in its methods, although it culminates in demanding the abolition of the class antagonism between bourgeoisie and proletariat.
> The socialists are thoroughly tame and peaceable, accept our existing order, bad as it is, so far as to reject all other methods but that of winning public opinion. . . . They bemoan the demoralisation of the lower classes. . . . They understand, it is true, why the working mass is resentful against the bourgeoisie, but regard as unfruitful this class hatred which is, after all, the only moral incentive by which the worker can be brought nearer the goal. They preach instead a philanthropy and universal love far more unfruitful for the present state of England. They acknowledge only a psychological development, a development of man in the abstract, and wholly isolated from all relation to the past, whereas the whole world rests upon that past, the individual man included. Hence they are too abstract, too metaphysical, and accomplish little.[2]

This excellent characterisation of British socialism Engels supplements with an analysis of Chartism and the differentiation which occurred in British Chartism after the bloody events of 1839–42. Engels supposed that true socialism might develop out of Chartism. The Chartists are theoretically the more backward, the less developed, but they are genuine proletarians, true representatives of their class.[3] However, as Engels himself afterwards wrote, these predictions did not come true. British socialism during the whole of the nineteenth century remained just as abstractly fruitless as the socialism of the 'fifties.

[1] Engels, *Condition of the Working Class in England.*
[2] *Ibid.*   [3] *Ibid.*

Marx studied the economics and the struggle of classes in England, and occupied himself thoroughly with the labour movement, which "instinctively grew out of the very relationships of production on both sides of the Atlantic Ocean." [1]

The trade unions are a weapon for the struggle against the capitalists, and therefore the creation of trade unions signifies a serious step forward for the working class—this idea penetrates the whole of Marx's *Capital*. Thus, for example, in an extensive description of the workers' struggle for shorter working hours, Marx writes:

> The formation since the close of 1865 of a trade union among the agricultural labourers, at first in Scotland, is a *historic* event. [2]

The great importance that Marx attached to the trade unions can be seen from the fact that he was the initiator of the idea of affiliating the trade unions to the First International and that he did very much in order to set up direct contacts with the local branches of the British trade unions. The attitude of some of the trade unions towards the First International can be seen from the following notes in the minutes of the General Council:

> On February 21, 1865, a letter from the bricklayers was read in the General Council in which the former expressed the desire to join the International. On March 28, 1865, the deputation of the General Council reported on its visit to the shoemakers' conference, which passed a resolution agreeing with the principles of the International Workingmen's Association and pledged to "endeavour to spread its liberal and glorious ideas among our constituents." On April 1, 1865, the Carpenters' Union of Chelsea asked that deputies be sent to explain the principles of the International Association. Weston communicated on the deputation to the Miners' Union. On April 3, 1866, the Executive Committee of the British Tailors' Union "expressed kind feeling toward the Association and a promise to join it." Then also the General Council heard a communication that the ribbon and small wares weavers of Coventry wished to join the I.W.A. On April 10, 1866, a communication was read that the West-End Bootmakers' Society had granted the General Council one pound

[1] Marx, *Capital*, Vol. I.
[2] *Ibid.*

and that they proposed to appoint Odger as a delegate to the Congress. On April 17, 1866, the Society was accepted as a branch of the International Workingmen's Association. Then also it was reported that Weston and Jung had been delegated to attend the meeting of the Plasterers Committee. On May 1, 1866, Jung reported on his and Lafargue's visit to the local branch of the Operative Bricklayers. They had been most enthusiastically received and were given promises of support. On May 15, 1866, the Darlington section of the Amalgamated Tailors' Union was admitted to the International. On July 17, 1866, a communication was read to the effect that the Hand-in-Hand Society of Coopers, who had agreed to join the International, assessed each member one shilling to defray the expenses of the Geneva Congress. At this same meeting it was reported that the meeting of cabinet-makers had been visited by a deputation from the International and had resolved to deduct one pound for defraying the expenses of the Congress. On August 17, 1866, a report was made that the London Society of Compositors had elected their secretary to the Geneva Congress. The Amalgamated Engineers' Society declined the proposal to send a delegate to the Congress and refused to give permission for a deputation to visit its branches.[1]

This excerpt from the minutes is quite characteristic, considering that it reflects the interest felt among some of the trade unions for the First International. In the organ of Johann Philipp Becker, *Vorbote*, of May 1866, mention is made of five big unions which had completely affiliated to the International (up till then only individual trade union members had affiliated to the International), namely: the silk-ribbon weavers' union, 1,000 members; the tailors' union, 8,000 members; the boot-makers' union, 9,000 members; the mechanics' union and the sieve-makers' union. In the July issue of that same magazine we read that the united delegates' meeting of cabinet-makers of England and Manchester (the chairman of the meeting was Applegarth) had unanimously decided to recommend all of their locals to join the International.

In this same way the masons' unions of London and Stratford joined the International, also many smaller societies, and finally, the Amalgamated Union of British Mechanics, with its mem-

[1] Minutes of the General Council of the International Workingmen's Association, Archives, Marx-Engels-Lenin Institute.

bership of 33,000. The November issue of *Vorbote* informs its readers of the affiliation to the International of the Basketmakers' Union of England (300 members) and the Navvy Workers' Union (28,000 members).[1]

In the report written by Marx to the Basle Congress, it is said that the following resolution had been adopted at the General Congress of British Trade Unions recently held in Birmingham:

> As the International Workingmen's Association endeavours to consolidate and extend the interests of the toiling masses, which are everywhere identical, this Congress heartily recommends that association to the support of the workingmen of the United Kingdom, especially of all organised bodies, and strongly urges them to become affiliated to that body believing that the realisation of its principles would also conclude lasting peace between the nations of the earth.[2]

But it must be borne in mind that many of the trade unions refused to affiliate to the International. Thus, for example, when the General Council of the International Workingmen's Association in October 1866 proposed that the London Trades Union Council affiliate to the International, and, in case of non-acceptance, that permission be granted the representatives of the International to come to its meeting and expound the views of the International Association, the London Trades Union Council refused. It is worth noting that at that time there was quite a large group of Englishmen in the General Council—Odger, Applegarth, Weston, Lucroft, etc., Odger being the President of the General Council. It is of interest also that Sydney and Beatrice Webb, historians of British trade unionism, in their two-volume *Industrial Democracy* do not devote *even one line* to the attitude of the British trade unions towards the First International, while in the *History of Trade Unionism* there is only one remark on this question.[3] But, in reality, we know that this question is no less important than the statutes of any union, or the opinion of bourgeois economists and British clergymen

[1] Gustav Jaeckh, *Die Internationale*, p. 13, Leipzig, 1904.
[2] Minutes of the General Council of the International Workingmen's Association, Archives, Marx-Engels-Lenin Institute.
[3] See Sydney and Beatrice Webb, *History of Trade Unionism*. New ed. 1902, pp. 217-18.

of the harm of trade unionism and the anti-religious character of the strike movement. However, these objective historians, who collected the statutes of all unions and the apprenticeship rules for several hundred years, who got out of the trade union archives material even of a secondary nature, did not seem to take note of the First International, which had its seat in London from 1864 to 1872. Such scientific blindness bears only too vividly a political character.

The Fabian historians of British trade unionism evidently thought that such a disdainful attitude towards Marx and the International Workingmen's Association would be bound to lessen the merits of Marx and the First International. But they were mistaken and only once again proved that Marx and the First International were feared all along by the "near-socialist" intelligentsia.

Engels brilliantly characterised Fabian socialism, for he had observed the development of socialist and pseudo-socialist ideas in England for many decades. Here is what he wrote on January 18, 1893, to Sorge:

> The Fabians here in London are a gang of careerists, who, however, have sense enough to realise the inevitability of a social revolution; but as they do not want to entrust this colossal work to the raw proletariat alone, they have deigned to take over its leadership. *Fear of the revolution is their main principle.*[1] They are 'intellectuals' *par excellence.* . . . Their socialism is municipal socialism; the commune, and not the nation, must, at least in the first stages, become the owner of the means of production. And their socialism they depict as the ultimate, but inevitable consequence of bourgeois liberalism. Hence their tactic: not to wage a determined fight against the Liberals as enemies; but to push them to socialist conclusions, *i.e.,* to hoodwink them, to permeate liberalism with socialism . . . not to run socialist candidates against the Liberals, but to palm the former off on the latter, *i.e.,* to have socialist candidates elected by fraud . . . and they do not, of course, understand that in playing this petty game they will either be deceived themselves or will defraud socialism.

> The Fabians have published, along with all kinds of trash, a few good propagandist works, and this is the best that was

---

[1] Italics mine.—*A.L.*

done in this sphere by the English. But as soon as they return to their specific tactics, the glossing over of the class struggle— things get bad. They hate Marx and all of us fanatically on account of the class struggle. . . .

This incisive characterisation of the Fabians explains also the scientific "impartiality" of the historians of the British labour movement. If "fear of the revolution is their basic principle," it is not a bit surprising that the Fabians fanatically hate Marx, for he was a most enthusiastic fighter for the proletarian revolution. It was not without good reason that the British bourgeois press called Marx the "Red Terror Doctor." [1]

The General Council of the First International was, as far as composition is concerned, heterogeneous to the extreme; a constant struggle was waged there on the main theoretical and political problems of the labour movement. The discussion organised by the General Council of the International Working-men's Association between Marx and Weston on the question of value, price and profit was very characteristic.

Early in November 1864, Marx wrote to Engels:

> An old Owenist, Weston, to-day himself a manufacturer, a very nice and pleasant old man, submitted a programme exceedingly verbose and terribly confused.[2]

This "nice and pleasant man" brought in much confusion, and the General Council resolved to organise a discussion on this controversial question. On May 20, 1865, Marx wrote to Engels:

> A special meeting of the International will be held to-night. A fine old scout, an old Owenist named Weston, a cabinet-maker, put up two points, which he had been constantly defending in *The Beehive*.
> (1) That a general rate in the rise of the rate of wages cannot be of any advantage to the workers;
> (2) that in view of this, etc., the trade unions have a *harmful* effect.
> If these two theses, in which *he alone* of all the members of our society believes, were adopted, we should be in a bad fix, both

[1] Marx-Engels, *Selected Letters* (German ed.), p. 401.
[2] Marx and Engels, *Letters, Collected Works* (German ed.), Part III, Vol. 3, p. 197.

on account of our local trade unions, as well as of the infection of strikes that has spread all over the Continent.

On this occasion—since non-members will be permitted to the meeting—he will receive the support of a lone Englishman, who wrote a pamphlet in this same spirit. I, of course, am expected to refute him.

Naturally, I know the two main points beforehand:
(1) That wages determine the value of commodities;
(2) that if the capitalists to-day pay five shillings instead of four, they will to-morrow (enabled to do so by the increased demand) sell their commodities for five shillings instead of four.[1]

The discussions between Marx and Weston were recorded in the minutes of the General Council as follows:

> On May 30, 1865, Weston read a paper on wages. Marx spoke, advancing his views, which were in contradiction with those of Weston. On June 27, 1865, Marx read the part of his report on wages in response to the report of Weston. On July 4, 1865, a debate was held on the question of the position of Weston and Marx.[2]

Much to our regret we do not have any details of the debates. However, we know what Marx said at these meetings. His report to the General Council on *Value, Price and Profit* corresponds to the chapter on this same subject in the first volume of *Capital*. Marx summed up Weston's views in the following two points:

> . . . firstly, that the *amount of national production* is a *fixed thing*, a *constant* quantity or magnitude, as the mathematicians would say; secondly, that the *amount of real wages*, that is to say, of wages as measured by the quantity of the commodities they can buy, is a *fixed* amount, a *constant* magnitude.[3]

This lean theory led to rich political conclusions. If changes in wages, increases or decreases, in no way influence the standard of living of the workers, then why waste money and energy on

---

[1] Marx and Engels, *Correspondence in the Socialist Movement of Marx and Engels,* April, 1913, p. 147.
[2] Minutes of General Council of I.W.A. Archives, Marx-Engels-Lenin Institute.
[3] Marx, *Value, Price and Profit,* p. 10 (Allen & Unwin).

organising trade unions, preparing strikes, etc.? We again have before us Lassalle's iron law clothed in the more learned frock of British bourgeois political economy. "The address Citizen Weston read to us might have been compressed into a nutshell," Marx said when he began his speech. And, indeed, as Marx kept on analysing the "theory" of Weston, it appeared that even the nutshell grew quite empty. Marx, analysing the sophisms of bourgeois political economy, which had been defended by "kind old Weston," draws the following theoretical and practical conclusions:

Firstly. A general rise in the rate of wages would result in a fall of the general rate of profit, but, broadly speaking, not affect the prices of commodities.

Secondly. The general tendency of capitalist production is not to raise, but to sink the average standard of wages.

Thirdly. Trade Unions work well as centres of resistance against the encroachments of capital. They fail partially from an injudicious use of their power. They fail generally from limiting themselves to a guerilla war against the effects of the existing system, instead of simultaneously trying to change it, instead of using their organised forces as a lever for the final emancipation of the working class, that is to say, the ultimate abolition of the wages system.[1]

To-day, fifty years after his death, this reply of Marx does not need any special commentary, for the ideas of Marx have become the property of millions. But imagine how difficult it must have been for Marx to carry on the discussion among the leadership of the International on a question which should have been absolutely clear to the leaders of the labour movement. If Marx did give such a scientific and seriously substantiated reply to Weston, it is because in all countries there had been much hesitation and confusion and many wrong theories precisely in connection with this question.

Naturally, the greater part of the British trade unions did not interest themselves with such problems and regarded the First International as an organisation not binding or compulsory for anyone. Marx and Engels saw how the leaders of the trade unions and the Chartist movement faded politically, how the

[1] *Value, Price and Profit*, pp. 93-94 (Allen & Unwin).

bourgeoisie succeeded in taming the trade unions, turning them into an appendage of their bourgeois parties. Hence the leadership of the British labour movement was sharply criticised. In connection with the circumstance that one of the leaders of the Chartist movement began to preach collaboration between the workers and the bourgeoisie, Marx wrote on November 24, 1857, in his letter to Engels:

> Jones plays a very silly part here, for as you know, long before the crisis he, without any definite intention other than to find a pretext for agitation during the period of quiet, planned the convocation of a Chartist conference. . . But now, instead of taking advantage of the crisis and replacing the poorly-planned pretext for agitation with real effective agitation, he sticks to his nonsense, shocks the workers with his preachments about collaboration with the bourgeoisie. . . .[1]

The "evolution" of Jones interested Marx and Engels very much. On October 7, 1858, Engels wrote to Marx:

> The story about Jones is quite disgusting—after hearing this story one would almost have to believe that the *British proletarian movement in its old traditionally Chartist form must completely perish before it can develop in a new life-sustaining form.* . . . Besides, it seems to me that Jones' new move in connection with the former more or less successful attempts at such an alliance is indeed connected with the fact *that the British proletariat is becoming more and more bourgeoisified,* so that this most bourgeois of all nations in the end apparently wants to have a bourgeois aristocracy and a bourgeois proletariat alongside the bourgeoisie. For a nation that exploits the whole world, this as a matter of fact is more or less natural.[2]

Already in this letter Engels raises the question of the influence of the bourgeoisie over the proletariat and the reasons why the British workers were becoming bourgeoisified. Both Marx and Engels repeatedly return to this question.

On February 11, 1878, Marx wrote to W. Liebnecht:

> Owing to the period of corruption which set in after 1848 the working class of England gradually became more and more

---

[1] Marx and Engels, *Letters.*
[2] Marx and Engels, *Collected Works* (German ed.) Part III, Vol. 2, p. 339.

demoralised and finally reached the state of a simple appendage of the "great" Liberal Party, *i.e.*, the party of their own enslavers —the capitalists. The leadership of the working class of England has wholly passed into the hands of the corrupted leaders of the trade unions and the professional agitators.[1]

Thus Marx established the definite period, when the decline of the revolutionary mood in the trade unions and in the labour movement of England began.

This coincided with the decline of the Chartist movement.

Some of the trade unions were rather sympathetic to the launching of the First International, but others from the very outset regarded the International only as a possible source of material aid in cases of strikes. On February 25, 1865, Marx wrote to Engels:

> As far as the London trade unions are concerned, we have a new affiliation every day, so that we shall become a force by and by. But henceforth also the difficulties will begin.[2]

The difficulties were these: that affiliation in no way proved that the trade unions had really come over to the platform of the First International. Marx realised this, yet he attached great significance to the affiliation of the trade unions to the International Workingmen's Association. On January 15, 1866, he wrote to Kugelmann:

> We have succeeded in drawing into the movement the one really big workers' organisation, the English Trade Unions, which formerly concerned themselves *exclusively* with wage questions.[3]

However, Marx understood that the trade unions had not said their last word by far, and that collisions with the leaders of the trade unions were inevitable. Because a rumour spread among the British trade unions that the International Workingmen's Association might render aid during strikes, some of the leaders, who had nothing at all to do with socialism, began to

---

[1] *Archives* of Marx and Engels, vol. V, p. 383, Marx-Engels-Lenin Institute, Moscow.
[2] Marx and Engels, *Collected Works* (German ed.), Part III, Vol. 3, p. 233.
[3] Marx, *Letters to Kugelmann*, with introduction by Lenin, p. 33. Martin Lawrence, Ltd.

run to the International. On September 11, 1867, Marx wrote
to Engels:

> These British scoundrels among the trade unionists, for whom
> we went too 'far' now come running up to us.[1]

What they came running for is clear. They were interested
in material aid only and nothing else. How Marx appraised
the leaders of the English trade unions can also be seen from his
letter to Kugelmann, in which he said the following:

> . . . In England at the moment only the rural labour move-
> ment shows any advance; the industrial workers have first of all
> to get rid of their present leaders. When I denounced them at the
> Hague Congress, I knew that I was letting myself in for unpopu-
> larity, slander, etc., but such consequences have always been a
> matter of indifference to me. Here and there people are beginning
> to see that in making that denunciation I was only doing my
> duty.[2]

Wherein lies the cause of this state of the trade unions in
England? Why did considerable sections of the workers become
more and more bourgeois?

In the works of Engels we find brilliant pages devoted to a
characterisation of the British labour movement. Here is what
Engels writes to Bernstein on June 17, 1878:

> The British labour movement is to-day and for many years has
> been working in a narrow circle of strikes for higher wages and
> shorter hours without finding a solution; besides, these strikes are
> looked upon not as an expedient and not as a means of propa-
> ganda and organisation but as an ultimate aim. The trade unions
> exclude on principle and by virtue of their statutes, all political
> action and consequently also the participation in the general
> activity of the working class as a class. The workers are divided
> politically into Conservatives and Liberal Radicals, into adherents
> of the ministry of Disraeli (Beaconsfield) and adherents of the
> Gladstone ministry. We can consequently speak about a labour
> movement here only in so far as strikes are waged here, which,
> whether successful or not, cannot lead the movement one step

[1] Marx and Engels, *Unedited letters in the Socialist Movement*, May-June,
1914, p. 288.
[2] Marx, *Letters to Kugelmann*. p. 135. Martin Lawrence, Ltd.

further. When such strikes, which moreover, during the last years of depression have often been called by the capitalists themselves, in order to have a pretext for closing down their factories, when such strikes, during which the working class does not move even one step forward, are magnified to the proportions of a world-historic struggle . . . then, in my opinion, this can only bring harm. We must not pass in silence over the fact that at the present moment no real labour movement, in the continental meaning of the word, exists here.[1]

Engels again returns to this question. To the question put by Kautsky, as to what the English workers thought of the colonial policy, Engels replies in his letter of September 12, 1882:

They think the same about this as *they think about politics in general,* the same that the bourgeoisie thinks about it. For there is no workers' party here, there are only Conservative and Liberal Radicals and the *workers also get their morale thanks to the British monopoly of the world and colonial markets.*[2]

The causes that led Great Britain to such a state cannot last for ever. The special position occupied by England on the world market must come to an end. Engels made the political upward swing of the labour movement of England dependent on the loss by that country of its monopolist position on the world market. In his letter to Bebel on August 20, 1883, Engels wrote:

But a real working-class movement will develop here—unless something unexpected happens—only when the workers will begin to feel that the British world monopoly has been broken. *Participation in the domination of the world market was and is the economic basis of the political nullity of the British workers.*[3] Dragging along at the tail-end of the bourgeoisie in the economic exploitation of this monopoly, but always sharing in its profits, they naturally, from the political point of view, drag along at the tail-end of the 'great Liberal Party' which has thrown them some small sops, recognises trade unions and the right to strike, gave up the struggle for the unlimited working day and gave the bulk of the higher-paid workers the right to vote. But if

[1] *Archives* of Marx and Engels, p. 136, Marx-Engels-Lenin Institute, Moscow, 1923.
[2] *Archives,* Marx and Engels, pp. 203-04.
[3] Italics mine.—*A.L.*

America and the joint competition of the other industrial countries make a considerable breech in this monopoly (as far as iron
is concerned, the time is not far off, but unfortunately in cotton
this is not yet the case), you will see things moving here.[1]

Engels correctly prophesied the beginning of the radical turn
in the labour movement of England; however, he could foresee
what deep root the monopoly of England would take among
the masses and how long and how dear the working class of
England would have to pay for the privileged position which
England had occupied for dozens of years on the world market.
The leaders of the trade unions not only were and are to-day
appendages of the bourgeois parties, but have turned into the
bitterest enemies of the growing revolutionary labour movement.
In his letter of December 8, 1882, Engels informs Marx about
the following interesting fact:

> *Apropos* the trade union deputation: when at the meeting
> of the 'Possibilists' the French had sung the *Marseillaise* in their
> honour, the honourable Shipton and his crew thought that they
> must meet the challenge and began to sing in unison 'God Save
> the Queen.'[2]

It is not surprising, then, that Marx and Engels felt hatred
for those leaders of the trade unions who led the trade unions
further and further away from their historical mission. He who
wants to understand the modern trade union movement of
England, the reasons why it lags behind and the methods of
overcoming this backwardness, should study attentively what
the founders of Marxism wrote about the bourgeoisification of
the British proletariat, about the first steps and the further
development of the trade unions.

---

[1] *Archives,* Marx and Engels, p. 225.
[2] Marx and Engels, *Collected Works* (German ed.) Part III, Vol. 4, p. 510.

CHAPTER V

Marx and the Labour Movement in France

FRENCH socialism, as is well known, constitutes one of the sources of Marxism. What did Marx really take from French socialism and what did he contribute to it? Marx attentively studied the French revolutions, beginning with the Great Revolution of 1789; the strikes, revolts, mass battles of the French proletariat, and how the class struggles and all movements of the worker and peasant masses were reflected in the different socialist systems (Socialist-Utopians, Communists, Utopians, Blanquists, Mutualists, Possibilists, Marxists, etc.). In the preface to the Cologne Trial of Communists, Engels wrote that he and Marx, leading the union of Communists, had followed the example of Marat. This most consistent bourgeois revolutionary attracted Marx and Engels by his iron will, revolutionary irreconcilability and revolutionary fearlessness. This is how proletarian revolutionaries were forged in the experiences acquired by the finest bourgeois revolutionaries.

Marx, studying the bourgeois revolutions of France, showed with the power so distinctive of him how the bourgeoisie utilised the workers as cannon-fodder, and how after every revolution it would direct all the forces of the new and old State apparatus against the working masses. Marx saw the utopianism of the programmes of Baboeuf, Saint Simon, Fourier and Cabet. However, he highly valued them as forerunners of scientific socialism. He knew how to draw the line between sincere utopian socialism and the petty-bourgeois socialist intrigues of Louis Blanc and company. Marx created scientific socialism by the dialectical negation of utopian socialism and by a graphic treatment of the stormy history of the revolutionary achievements of the French toiling masses. The revolutionary experiences of the masses are precisely the major and basic French source of Marxism.

63

The Conspiracy of the Equals was the reply given to the victory of the Thermidorian reaction by the masses whom the Great Revolution had deceived. The Baboeuvians expressed their views in four documents: (1) The Manifesto of the Equals; (2) the Analysis of Doctrines; (3) the Act of Revolts; and (4) the Decrees. The Baboeuvians aimed at organising a revolt of the poor against the rich; they realised that the root of all evil lay in private property and therefore they fought for economic equality. The Manifesto of the Equals proclaimed that the "French Revolution was only the forerunner of another greater, more powerful revolution, which was bound to be also the last." The programme of the Baboeuvians was in its day a tremendous leap forward, and, although Baboeuf and the Baboeuvians failed to see the social force that would actually be able to carry out their programme in fact (and therein lies their utopianism), yet this communist programme reflected the great forward moves among the masses, who had derived no advantage from the many years of revolutionary upheavals.

The suppression of the Conspiracy of the Equals and the victory of Napoleon over the foreign and domestic enemies gave rise to a certain amount of depression in the ranks of the masses. Socialist ideas began to come to the forefront in the form of semi-religious and semi-socialist teachings. The aristocrat Saint Simon and the rank and file citizen Charles Fourier came out with their plans for reorganising humanity. The beneficial part of their preachings lies not in their plans for a happy future, but in the criticisms of the present and in the emphasis laid on the antagonism between the wealthy and the poor. But no matter how Saint Simon and Charles Fourier differed in origin and plans, both of them issued their appeals to the "hearts of men," and hoped to win the progressive capitalists over to their side and by peaceful means to reorganise human reason that had gone off the proper track.

Neither of these utopians wanted even to hear of a revolution. In view of the fact that Saint Simon and Fourier did not see the social force that could realise their dreams, they appealed to the powers of the next world, to religion, which played quite a considerable part in their teachings. The disciples of Saint Simon and Fourier developed the mystic side of the teachings of these great utopians to an even greater extent. Bazard, Enfantin,

Victor Considerant, Pièrre Leroux, etc., attempted under new conditions to develop the mystical-utopian part of the teachings of the great utopians and this is why they were attacked in the Communist Manifesto. Marx and Engels, while establishing the fact that the works of Baboeuf "express the demands of the proletariat," write the following about the utopians.

> The founders of these systems see, indeed, the class antagonisms, as well as the action of the decomposing elements in the prevailing form of society. But the proletariat, as yet in its infancy, offers to them the spectacle of a class without any historical initiative or any independent political movement.
>
> Since the development of class antagonism keeps even pace with the development of industry, the economic situation, as they find it, does not as yet offer to them the material conditions for the emancipation of the proletariat. They therefore search after a new social science, after new social laws that are to create these conditions. . . .
>
> The undeveloped state of the class struggle, as well as their own surroundings, cause Socialists of this kind to consider themselves far superior to all class antagonisms. They want to improve the condition of every member of society, even that of the most favoured. Hence, they habitually appeal to society at large, without distinction of class; nay, by preference to the ruling class. . . .
>
> Hence, they reject all political, and especially all revolutionary action; they wish to attain their ends by peaceful means, and endeavour, by small experiments, necessarily doomed to failure, and by the force of example, to pave the way for the new social gospel.[1]

The appraisal of the French utopians given by Engels in his famous *Anti-Dühring* is extremely interesting. Emphasising the backward economic relations in France at the beginning of the nineteenth century, Engels wrote:

> As early as his *Geneva Letters* Saint Simon laid down the principle that 'all men ought to work.' When he wrote this work he already knew that the reign of terror was the reign of the propertyless masses. . . . But to conceive of the French Revolution as a class war between nobility, bourgeoisie and *propertyless*

---

[1] *Communist Manifesto*, pp. 35-36 (Martin Lawrence, London; International Publishers, New York).

masses was, indeed in the year 1802, the discovery of genius. . . .

In Fourier we find a critique of existing social conditions which, typically French in its wit, is none the less penetrating. (Italics mine.—*A.L.*)[1]

From this we can see why Marx and Engels valued the utopians. For them it was important that the utopians had spoken a new word in their time concerning the interests of the poor, that they saw the class contradictions, etc. Marx and Engels took quite another attitude towards the disciples of these utopians, who dragged the movement backward, and desired to remain at the stage already traversed. In the *Communist Manifesto* we read the following about them:

> . . . although the originators of these systems were, in many respects, revolutionary, their disciples have, in every case, formed mere reactionary sects. They hold fast by the original views of their masters, in opposition to the progressive historical development of the proletariat. They, therefore, endeavour, and that consistently, to deaden the class struggle and to reconcile the class antagonisms. . . . By degrees they sink into the category of the reactionary conservative Socialists depicted above, differing from these only by more systematic pedantry, and by their fanatical and superstitious belief in the miraculous effects of their social science.
>
> They, therefore, violently oppose all political action on the part of the working class; such action, according to them, can only result from blind unbelief in the new gospel.[2]

The communist-utopian Etienne Cabet also very little resembled his predecessor Baboeuf. Whereas Baboeuf prepared a revolt and wanted to rouse the masses against those who utilised the revolution for acquiring more wealth, Etienne Cabet dreamt of creating a communist society without any struggle. His *Voyage en Icarie* ends with the following words: "If I held the revolution in the hollow of my hand, I would release it even if I had to die in banishment for it." The fear of revolution is bred here by the disappointment in past revolutions, which had all ended unfavourably for the working class.

[1] Engels, *Anti-Dühring* (German edition), p. 277.
[2] *Communist Manifesto,* p. 37.

And what is the attitude of all these theoreticians of the first half of the nineteenth century towards Marx and Marxism? Some writers believed that Marxism represented the summation of the ideas of Saint Simon, Fourier and their disciples. This conclusion was drawn also by the French socialist Paul Louis, who wrote the following on the subject:

> Louis Blanc and Vidal pointed to the necessity of having recourse to State power and claimed the principle of the seizure of public power to be the necessary preliminary condition of every revolution. Beker and Cabet were the first to deal in detail with collectivism and communism. Finally, Proudhon vividly described the contradictions of class interests, indicated the shortcomings of private property, the constant exploitation by the capitalist of the hired worker, exposed the internal contradictions of the economic system, which breeds the more unfortunates the more riches it creates. Gathering all of these together, we get almost the complete expression of Marxism.[1]

Only a typical eclectic, a person who tried to combine his membership in the Communist Party of France with contributions to the Yellow Press, could come to the conclusion that the theories of Louis Blanc, Vidal, Becker and Proudhon in their totality are "almost equal to Marxism." Paul Louis makes the reservation that all of these philosophers were imbued with the spirit of idealism but that they had not reached historical materialism; however, he does not consider the latter to be very important, since "historical materialism does not comprise an indivisible part of the laws of Marxian theory." Can it be said that all the viewpoints of the socialist-utopians, communist-utopians and petty-bourgeois socialists of the type of Proudhon and Louis Blanc constitute "near-Marxism"? By no means. This would mean failure to understand the difference between Marxism and all of the French socialist teachings of that period. Of course, Marx critically studied all that had been created in the field of socialist ideas in France, but what new elements did Marx bring, in comparison with these ideas?

(1) Marx considered the proletariat to be the only force that would successfully fight for socialism. (2) Marx drew a sharp

[1] Paul Louis, *French Thinkers and Statesmen of the Nineteenth Century* (Russian edition), Moscow, 1905, pp. 58-59.

political line between the proletariat and other classes. (3) Marx believed revolution by force and the establishment of the dictatorship of the proletariat to be the only path towards socialism.

Only one socialist who began his labour during the first half of the nineteenth century was considered by Marx to be a proletarian revolutionary. This was Auguste Blanqui. Blanqui seethed with deep hatred against the oppressors and, although he was far from really understanding scientific socialism and built his plans not on mass demonstrations but on the actions of a small group of conspirators, Marx considered Blanqui to be the greatest communist-revolutionary after Baboeuf and called him a leader of the proletarian party.

Marx saw the internal class mechanism of the French revolutions. He wrote:

> Just as the workers in the July days (1830—*A.L.*) had fought and beat the *bourgeois monarchy,* so in the February days (1848—*A.L.*) they fought and beat the bourgeois republic. Just as the July Monarchy had to proclaim itself a monarchy surrounded by republican institutions, so the February Republic was forced to proclaim itself a *republic surrounded by social institutions.* The Paris proletariat compelled this concession too.[1]

But the workers were only formally satisfied.

> "On February 23, at about noon," Daniel Stern relates, "a large number of corporations, with about twelve thousand persons, came out on to Greve Square and stood in deep silence. On their banners inscriptions could be seen: Organisation of Labour, Labour Ministry, Abolish Exploitation of Man by Man."[2]

The first two demands of the workers, formulated by socialists of the type of Louis Blanc, called forth the following ironical remark from Marx:

> *Organisation of Labour:* But wage labour is the existing bourgeois organisation of Labour. Without it there is no capital, no bourgeoisie, no bourgeois society. *Their own Ministry of Labour!*

[1] Marx, *Class Struggle in France.* Martin Lawrence, p. 41.
[2] Daniel Stern, *History of the French Revolution,* 1848 (Russian edition), Vol. 1, p. 287.

But the Ministries of Finance, of Trade, of Public Works, aren't these the bourgeois labour ministries? [1]

The provisional government cleverly turned the tables, by replying to the demands of the workers with the appointment of the Luxemburg Commission, where Louis Blanc and Albert made long speeches about the future, and drew the minds of the workers away from the present. In the primitive demands of the workers and in the Luxemburg Commission itself Marx saw a reflection of the class struggle.

> The right to work—is the first clumsy formula embracing the revolutionary demands of the proletariat.[2]

> To the Luxemburg Commission, this creation of the Paris workers, remains the merit of having disclosed from the European tribune the secret of the revolution of the nineteenth century: the *emancipation of the proletariat*.[3]

The Paris proletariat suffered defeat in the July days, because politically and organisationally it had not risen to the level of its historical tasks. Marx, in his brilliant analysis of the disposition of class forces in the revolution of 1848, wrote:

> A class in which the revolutionary interests of society are concentrated, so soon as it has risen up, finds directly in its own situation the content and the material of its revolutionary activity; foes to be laid low, measures dictated by the needs of the struggle to be taken; the consequences of its own deeds drive it on. It makes no theoretical inquiries into its own task. The French working class had not attained this standpoint; it was still incapable of accomplishing its own revolution.[4]

But in order that the working class can make a *revolution for itself*, not only is a certain level of political consciousness and organisation necessary, but there must be a special disposition of class forces in the given country. Here is what Marx writes:

> The French workers could not take a step forward, could not touch a hair of the bourgeois order before the course of the revolution had forced the masses of the nation, the peasants and

[1] Marx, *Class Struggle in France*, p. 48.
[2] *Ibid.*, p. 44.   [3] *Ibid.*, p. 42.   [4] *Ibid.*, p. 42.

petty bourgeois, standing between the proletariat and *the bourgeoisie* and in revolt not against this order, against the rule of capital, to attach itself to the proletariat, as its vanguard. The workers could only buy this victory through the huge defeat of June.[1]

It is precisely this specific disposition of class forces that defined the nature of the socialist system. This is what gave rise to bourgeois and petty-bourgeois socialism,

> which was the theoretical expression of the proletariat only so long as it had not yet developed further into a free historical self-movement.[2]

While this socialism went over from the proletariat to the petty bourgeoisie. . .

> . . . the *proletariat* rallies more and more round *revolutionary* Socialism, around Communism, for which the bourgeoisie has itself found the name of Blanqui. This Socialism is the declaration of the permanence of the revolution, the class dictatorship of the revolution, the class dictatorship of the proletariat as the inevitable transit point to the abolition of class differences generally, to the abolition of all the productive relationships on which they rest, to the abolition of all social relations that correspond to these relationships of production, to the revolutionising of all the ideas that result from these social relations.[3]

This is how Marx in 1848 put the question of socialist tendencies and their *rôle* in the struggle of the French proletariat, and the causes of the June defeat. Many years later, in 1890, Engels in his preface to the *Communist Manifesto* said that already before the February Revolution of 1848 a sharp line of demarcation could have been observed between the socialists and communists. Engels writes the following on the subject:

> However, the section of the working class which, convinced that mere political revolution was not enough, demanded radical reconstruction of society—that section then called itself *Communist*. It was a still rough-hewn, only instinctive and frequently some-

---

[1] Marx, *Class Struggle in France*, p. 44.
[2] *Ibid.*, p. 125.   [3] *Ibid.*, p. 126.

what crude Communism. . . . Socialism in 1847 stood for a bourgeois movement, Communism for a working class movement.[1]

The smashing of the Paris proletariat in June, 1848, was the starting point of a lengthy period of reaction, not only in France, but all over the continent of Europe. The political defeat called forth ideological reaction—this is what caused the success of the idea to renounce the political struggle and to turn towards mutualism.

What is the political essence of Proudhonist mutualism? It is the idea of replacing the class struggle by mutual services, mutual aid, etc.; it is precisely what the bourgeoisie wanted from the working class in France, "tainted" by several revolutions.

After the bloody suppression of the June uprising the labour movement of France began to develop again, but with great difficulty. The attempts to solve the social problem by mutualism, by workers' banks, by organising communist settlements in the United States, were made parallel with the sharpening of the economic struggle for the vital needs and demands of the workers. The beginning of the 'sixties was noted by an upsurge. The Government of Napoleon III tried, along with repressions, to have recourse to demogogy. The Government encouraged the workers to send their representatives to international exhibitions and tried to check the activities of the different working-class organisations (trade unions, mutual aid societies, industrial work-men's associations, mutual credit societies, workers' resistance societies, etc.) which despite their primitive political programmes and organisational weakness, were centres for gathering the forces of the working class.

In 1862 two workers' candidates came up in the elections; in 1864 an election platform-manifesto appeared, signed by sixty workers, representatives of various working-class organisations. The Government continued its manœuvres. It undertook to de-fray the expenses of the trip of 200 workers to the international exhibition in London. The Government began to subsidise some of the mutual aid societies; finally, the law of May 25, 1864, gave the workers the right of association. That this concession was merely formal can be seen from the fact that strikers con-tinued to be persecuted. Up till 1864 there had been about

[1] *Communist Manifesto*, p. 45.

seventy strike trials a year, while after the promulgation of the law on the "right to strike" fifty-one trials were held during the year for "infringing the freedom of labour."

The trip to England in 1862 made a great impression on the delegates, and the reports of these delegates played an important political and organisational part. Of particularly great significance was the exchange of greetings between the French and British workers in connection with this trip—it was the concrete beginning of the establishment of international contacts. While the year 1862 was only a beginning in this direction, the trip of the French workers' delegation in 1864 was the starting point for the foundation of the International Workingmen's Association, which played such a tremendous *rôle* in spreading the ideas of Marx and Engels, in the establishment of the organisation which during the course of nine years (1864-1872) served as the beacon light for the toiling masses of Europe and America and the hobgoblin of the international bourgeoisie.

Marx, as I have already said, was the soul of the First International; he saw better than anyone else the low theoretical and political level of the national sections, especially of the French section. But the International was created precisely for raising the level of its integral parts. The French workers brought their rich revolutionary traditions into the First International; however, along with this they infused into the International also petty-bourgeois, socialist, semi-socialist and Proudhonist ideas, which were caught up by Bakunin and which finally led to the falling apart of the International Workingmen's Association.

The French workers met the creation of the International with tremendous interest. During the years of 1864 to 1870 the International developed into a force in France. Sections of the International multiplied all over the country and were quite variegated in composition. In all corners of France local unions, resistance societies, mutual aid societies, political groups, men and women workers on strike affiliated to the International Workingmen's Association. "The success of the Association surpassed all expectations here, in Paris, in Belgium, in Switzerland and in Italy," Marx wrote to Krugelmann on February 23, 1865.

First of all let us see how the labour movement in France was reflected in the Minutes of the International Workingmen's

Association. Here is what we read in the Minutes of the General Council:

On June 20, 1865, a report was read to the effect that the Lille Weavers' Society would most likely join the I.W.A. On July 4, 1865, a letter was read from Lyons confirming the receipt of 400 membership books and making further inquiries about the manufacture of tulle. It is stated that the strike ended unfavourably for the workers, "who had been compelled to succumb for lack of means of subsistence." On September 28, 1869, a letter was read from Marseilles announcing a lock-out of basket-makers and requesting assistance. The Secretary was instructed to reply that there was no prospect of financial help. The Secretary was also instructed to write to London basket-makers. On October 12, 1869, a letter from Obery of Rouen was read announcing a strike of the wool-spinners of Elboeuf and asking for aid. The spinners insisted upon a list of prices being fixed. Other towns joined in making this demand, and would strike in a fortnight if the demand was not granted. On October 26, 1869, a report was made on the trial of the delegates of 27 Paris trade unions against the bloody deeds at Aubain—34 killed and 36 wounded. Then also a report was heard on the miners' struggle in France. On November 2, 1869, the carpenters of one Geneva shop were on strike against overtime. The French Government furnished charity girls to replace linen drapers' assistants on strike against Sunday work. On November 9 Jung reported that 2,000 Paris gilders resolved not to work longer than 10 hours a day under any circumstances. The society of Paris lithographers, having 300 members, and the Paris tin-plate workers, having 200 members, joined the I.W.A. On November 11, 1870, a letter was read from Neuville-sur-Saône asking for help for the cotton printers on strike. The Secretary was instructed to communicate with Manchester concerning the strike. The surgical instrument workers of Paris on strike applied for help. The Council agreed to assist by applying to the kindred trades at Sheffield. On April 6, 1870, Marx expressed the desire that the publication of the appeal in connection with the trial in Creuzot be postponed. Funds had been sent by everybody, and it would make a bad impression if London were to limit itself to words only. On April 10, 1870, a letter was read from Varlin in Paris to the effect that he had been in Lille for the purpose of organising a trade union section under the control of the International Workingmen's Association. The Federal Council could take over the leadership of the different trade union societies. Dupont calls the attention of the Council to the brutal sentences given the miners, who had been imprisoned in connection with the strike in Creuzot, and proposed that the Council issue an appeal. Dupont and Marx were charged to draw up this appeal. On May 31, 1870, the meeting heard a report of the delegate from the iron founders of Paris then on strike. It was proposed that the Council facilitate the task of the delegate to set up contracts with the trade societies by appointing a deputation to accompany him. Jung and Hales were appointed.[1]

However, this does not give a complete picture of the relations between the French workers and the First International. In his letters to Engels, Kugelmann and others, Marx very often refers to French affairs, not sparing strong words. The activities and manifestations of the Proudhonists agitated him very much, for he saw here the influence of the bourgeoisie over the proletariat. On October 9, 1866, Marx wrote to Kugelmann:

> The Parisian gentlemen have their heads full of the emptiest Proudhonist phrases. They babble about science and know nothing. They scorn all *revolutionary* action . . . *i.e.,* action arising out of the class struggle itself, all concentrated social movements, and therefore all those which can be carried through by *political* means (*e.g.,* the *legal* limitation of the working day).
> Under the pretext of freedom and anti-governmentalism, anti-authoritarian-individualism, these genetlemen, who for sixteen years have so calmly endured the most miserable despotism, and still endure it, actually preach the ordinary bourgeois sciences, only Proudhonistically idealised! [2]

Marx hated stage revolutionaries and melodramatic heroes. In his letters he especially attacks the London Section, consisting of French emigrants. In his letter to Kugelmann dated December 5, 1868, Marx declared that this section consisted of loafers and all sorts of riff-raff; "besides," he writes, "we are, of course, considered reactionaries by these strike-breakers." Here also he brilliantly characterises Felix Pyat:

> . . . A ship-wrecked fourth-rate French author of melodramas, and who in the revolution of '48 was only used as a toastmaster . . . and who has a perfect monomania for 'shouting in a

[1] Minutes of General Council of International Workingmen's Association. Archives. Marx-Engels-Lenin Institute.
[2] Marx, *Letters to Kugelmann,* p. 40.

whisper' and playing the dangerous conspirator. . . . Pyat wanted to use this gang to make the International Workingmen's Association a tool of his. He was particularly anxious to compromise us. At a public meeting which the French branch proclaimed and trumpeted in large placards as a meeting of the 'International Association,' Louis Napoleon, alias, Badinguet, was solemnly *condemned to death* . . . the execution of the sentence, of course, being left to the nameless Brutuses of Paris. . . .

We had the satisfaction of seeing that Blanqui got one of his friends to ridicule Pyat, also in the *Cigale,* leaving him the alternative of being recognized either as a monomaniac or a police agent.[1]

But Marx was mostly interested in developing the movement in the country. He attentively followed up the movement of the masses and systematically shared his impressions and views with his friends. On January 13, 1869, Marx wrote to Engels:

The strikes in Rouen, Vienne, etc. (cotton spinning industry), are about 6--7 weeks old. What is interesting here is the fact that shortly before this a general congress of the master manufacturers (and spinners) was held in Amiens under the chairmanship of the Mayor of Amiens. Here it was decided to compete with the English in England, etc. This was to be accomplished by means of FURTHERING LOWERING WAGES, after it had been admitted that only low wages (lower relative to English wages) made it possible to resist British competition in France itself. And actually after this meeting in Amiens wage-cuts began to be carried out in Rouen, Vienne, etc. Hence the strikes. We, of course, informed these people through Dupont of the bad state of affairs here (especially in the cotton trade) and of the difficulty in connection with this method of collecting funds AT THE PRESENT TIME. Meanwhile, as you will see from the enclosed letter (from Vienne) the strike in Vienne has ended. To the Rouen workers, where the conflict is still continuing, we for the time being ordered twenty pounds to be paid by the Paris bronze workers, who owed us this sum even before the time they were locked out. Generally speaking, these French workers act much more reasonably than the Swiss workers, and are at the same time much more modest in their demands.[2]

[1] *Ibid.*

[2] Marx to Engels, January 13, 1869. *Collected Works* (German edition), Part III, Vol. 4, pp. 48-49.

The situation in France at that time became more and more complicated every day. The revolution approached, and it is a fact that when scenting a revolution the liberal-democratic loons shout the loudest. On November 29, 1869, Marx wrote to Kugelmann:

> In France things are going well so far. On the one hand, the out-of-date demagogic and democratic bawlers of all shades are compromising themselves. On the other, Bonaparte is being driven along a path of concessions, on which he is certain to break his neck.[1]

On March 3, 1869, Marx wrote an extensive letter to Kugelmann in which he analysed the situation in France. From a number of symptoms Marx foresaw the approaching storm:

> A very interesting movement is going on in France [he wrote]. *The Parisians are making a regular study of their recent revolutionary past,* in order to prepare themselves for the business of the impending new revolution. And so the whole historic witches' cauldron is bubbling. . . . When shall we be so far?[2]

As I said above, Marx was chiefly anxious about whether the sections of the International would be able to rise to the occasion. Every time that the workers in France broke with Proudhonist traditions, Marx noted it as an important achievement. On May 18, 1870, he wrote to Engels:

> Our members in France demonstrate to the French Government *ad oculos* [before their eyes.—ED.] the difference between a political secret society and a real labour association. It had hardly succeeded in locking behind prison doors all the members of the Paris, Lyons, Rouen, Marseilles and other committees (some of them have fled to Switzerland and Belgium), when new committees, numerically twice as strong, announced in the newspapers that they were carrying on as successors of the old ones, and made the most insolent and defiant declarations, giving their home addresses to boot. The French Government has finally done what we so long desired, it has turned the political ques-

[1] Marx, *Letters to Kugelmann,* p. 97.
[2] *Ibid,* p. 89.

tion—Empire or Republic—into a question *de vie ou de mort* [of life or death.—Ed.] for the working class.[1]

Events reached a boiling point on July 19, 1870—the beginning of the Franco-Prussian War. From the very first days of the war the erstwhile rapidly rising tide of the labour movement receded violently; however, the movement was not smashed.

A number of French and German working-class organisations came out against the war. The *Reveil* published a manifesto against war addressed "To the workers of all countries." Three days after the declaration of war, on July 22, the section of the International in Neuilly-sur-Seine published an appeal strongly protesting against the war:

> Is it just a war? No! Is it a national war? No! It is merely a dynastic war. In the name of humanity, of democracy and the true interests of France, we adhere completely and emphatically to the protest of the International against the war.[2]

As early as July 23, the General Council of the First International issued an appeal against the war. This manifesto, written by Marx, condemns Napoleon and Bismarck, exposes these organisers of the Franco-Prussian War. This manifesto contains a prophetic phrase:

> Whatever may be the issue of Louis Bonaparte's war with Prussia, the death knell of the Second Empire has already sounded in Paris.[3]

This prophecy very soon became a reality. At the beginning of September, 1870, Napoleon surrendered with his army at Sedan and on September 4 a revolution broke out. The "National Defence Government," which, according to Marx, consisted of a "gang of ambitious lawyers," was visited on that day by a deputation from the Paris sections of the International and the Federation of Workers' Unions—a deputation thus representing the working class of Paris. It proposed a programme

---

[1] Marx and Engels, *Complete Works* (German edition), Part III, Vol. 4, p. 330.
[2] *First Appeal of the General Council in Connection with the Franco-Prussian War.* Marx and Engels, *Selected Works.*
[3] *Ibid.*

to the National Defence Government, on the adoption of which the confidence of the Parisian proletariat in the new government and the extent to which it would support the new government would depend. The chief demands of the programme were: the rule of the city of Paris was to be handed over to the population, which was to organise National Guards as well as elect judges from among its ranks; there was to be full freedom of the Press, amnesty and the separation of the Church from the State. The clique that had seized power (Thiers, Jules Favre and others) replied vaguely to these demands. In response to this the workers immediately organised a *vigilance committee* to watch the moves of the government. From the very outset the National Defence Government and the Paris proletariat expressed lack of confidence in each other. The class instinct of the workers told them that they had to deal with a government of national treachery, which feared the workers a thousand times more than it did the Prussians. On September 9, the International Workingmen's Association issued a new appeal, in which it exposed the imperialist cravings of Prussia, screened by the word "security" (what a modern word!—*A.L.*) and excellently characterised the Republic of Thiers, Jules Favre and other agents of the French bourgeoisie.

This Republic, Marx writes, did not overthrow the throne, it simply occupied the empty seat. . . . It inherited from the Empire not only a heap of ruins, but also its fear of the working class.

This remarkable characterisation of the republic of Thiers was confirmed within a few months. But at that time, several days after the overthrow of Napoleon, Marx believed that the workers would refrain from overthrowing the Government of September 4. "Every attempt to overthrow the new Government," Marx writes, "at the moment when the enemy practically knocks at the doors of Paris, would be insanity due to despair." In spite of this, the Blanquists did make a few attempts to overthrow the Government both on October 8 and 31, 1870, and January 29, 1871, but these attempts failed—the masses of the Paris population did not support them. Only when the betrayal of the Government became a fact, when the Government tried to disarm the National Guards, did the toiling masses rise —"did the glorious workers' revolution exercise untrammelled rule in Paris" (Marx). The Paris Commune, this forerunner of the Land of the Soviets, in spite of the prodigies of courage and self-sacrifice, lasted only two months. The Commune fell under the blows of the united reaction, the united front of the "hereditary enemies" which only yesterday had fought with one another: it fell because the Blanquists and Proudhonists who headed the Commune were groping their way and did not display the firmness and determination required at such a moment. There was good reason for the proposals the Commune made several times to Thiers, to exchange Cardinal Dorbois for Blanqui. Thiers refused, saying this would mean giving rebellious Paris a whole army corps. "Thiers rejected this idea," Marx writes, "for he knew that in the person of Blanqui he would give the Commune a head." When the Commune was proclaimed Marx immediately enlisted in the defence of this workers' government. Though he had been against the seizure of power, he did not argue, become sententious, he saw before him not only an uprising, but also the working class in power, and considered it to be the duty of a revolutionary not to reason but to help. In his letter to Kugelmann dated April 12, 1871, Marx enthusiastically writes about the heroism of the Communards, who stand "prepared to storm the heavens," criticises them for their lack of determination and declares that "if they are defeated nothing but their generosity will be to blame." Marx saw the weaknesses of the Commune, weaknesses which could not easily be overcome by advice. The International could not give the Commune what it lacked.

The Commune was smashed. "Order" was enthroned in triumph on the bones of the tens of thousands of murdered proletarians. The First International issued an appeal in connection with the civil war in France. In this document Marx manifested his unbounded hatred for the exploiters, exhibited the great passion and ardour of a great revolutionary. It is not simply an appeal, it is a political document that illumines the path of struggle of the working class for its dictatorship. Marx looks upon the Commune as a new type of government, the very birth of which is linked up with the destruction of the old order. "The Commune should not have been a parliamentarian, but a working corporation." It is well known that this idea of destroying the old State and creating a new type of State served as a basis not only for the theoretical works of Lenin (*State and Revolution*), but also for the practical activities in building the Soviet Republic.

Marx realised that it is impossible to demand much of a government that held power for only two months, and he therefore sharply polemised against those who tried to belittle the significance of the Commune or (after it was over) to crow about its inevitable defeat.

The great social achievement of the Commune, Marx wrote, *was its own existence,* its activity. The separate measures undertaken by it could indicate only *the direction in which the government of the people develops through the medium of the people themselves.*

In reply to a letter of Kugelmann, in which the latter stated that the Commune had had no chance of success, and that under such circumstances nothing should have been started (recollect the words of Plekhanov on the December uprising of 1905 in Moscow, "no arms should have been resorted to!"), Marx wrote back to him on April 17, 1871:

> World history would indeed be very easy to make if the struggle were taken up only on condition of infallibly favourable chances. . . . Whatever the immediate results may be, a new point of departure of world-historical importance has been gained.[1]

The proletariat of Paris paid very dearly for the attempt to build its own workers' State. The crushing of the Commune bled the working class white and caused it to remain aloof from politics for some time. The French sections of the International were shot down and smashed, and finally dissolved in 1872, by special decree. At that time the moderates of all shades and colours, who had left the ranks of the International out of fear of the revolution and had taken up a waiting attitude during the Commune, began to manifest activity among the workers. Barberet organised a "workers' trade union club." This club aimed at "realising co-ordination and justice by educational means" and at convincing public opinion of the "moderateness which the workers were manifesting in stating their rights." [2] In

[1] Marx, *Letters to Kugelmann.*
[2] Ferdinand Pelloutier, *History of the Labour Exchange,* 1921.

spite of the persecution of even these innocent clubs and societies they grew and multiplied. The workers once again began to take part in international exhibitions, and by 1875 there were in France 135 trade unions, which already began to discuss the idea of convening a workers' congress. The first workers' congress was held in Paris in 1876 with a very limited programme. As an antidote to the revolutionary ideas and slogans of the Commune, the problems here raised dealt with mutual aid, industrial associations, etc. The delegates to the Congress did not even think of planning to overthrow the bourgeois order; they merely wanted to touch it up a bit, to improve it; they wanted to "balance the relations between capital and labour, both in production and in consumption." Along with civil war, they condemned strikes, "which deal their blows at the strong and destroy the weak." [1]

The next workers' congress was held in 1877 in Lyons. Here some new moods were already observable. Here anarchist and collectivist speeches were heard. However, the bulk of the delegates occupied a moderate platform.

An altogether different mood dominated at the Marseilles Congress in 1879. Here it was evident that the working class was again beginning to gain strength, after the fall of the Paris Commune. The influence of the Marxian paper, *Egalité*, established by Jules Guesde in 1877, was felt. Lombard, secretary of the organisational committee for convening the Marseilles Congress, proposed to call this congress the "Socialist Workers' Congress of France." This proposal was unanimously adopted. The speakers came out openly against Louis Blanc and his theories. Whereas the Paris workers' congress had not even wanted to hear of the Communards, the Marseilles Congress sent the following reply to the greetings of the London exiles:

> Your approval has gratified all members of the Marseilles Socialist Workers' Congress. The delegates gathered here once again declare that they hold dear the principles for which you fought and suffered.[2]

The congress served as the starting point for the renaissance

---

[1] See Leon Blum, *Congresses of French Workers and Socialists in France, 1876--1900* (Russian edition), Moscow, 1906, pp. 7--8.
[2] *Ibid.*, p. 23, and Ferdinand Pelloutier, *History of the Labour Exchange.*

F

of the political movement, for at this congress a workers' party was founded which absorbed various elements. Marx played a very active *rôle* in drawing up the programme of this workers' party. Engels, in his letter to Bernstein dated October 25, 1881, wrote in detail how Marx, in the presence of Lafargue and himself, dictated to Guesde the basic points of the programme. What is most important in this programme approved by Marx? Against what did Benoit Malon and his adherents come out so energetically? Here are the chief points of the programme:

> whereas the emancipation of the producing class means simultaneously also the emancipation of all people, regardless of sex or race; and whereas the producers can be free only if they possess the means of production; and
>
> whereas there exist only two forms in which the means of production can belong to them: (1) individual form of possession, which never has existed generally, and which is being crowded out more and more by industrial progress; (2) collective form of ownership, the material and intellectual elements of which are created by the very development of the capitalist society; and
>
> whereas the second form can only be the result of the struggle of the organised working class, and whereas all the means at the disposal of the proletariat must be applied to realise this organisation including also general suffrage, which, thanks to this, will be converted from the weapon of deceit that it was before into a weapon of emancipation,
>
> therefore the French socialist workers, aiming in economic activity to socialise all means of production, resolve to take part in elections, as a means towards organisation and struggle. . . .

The question of elections was a serious problem for the labour movement of France of that period. On the one hand anti-parliamentarian and non-political opinions were very strong among the workers, and on the other hand, many had an exaggerated notion of the saving power of the ballot and the possibility of emancipating the working class by peaceful means. Therefore, the programme of the Workers' Party contained a special chapter devoted to the *rôle* of the election campaigns in the general class struggle of the proletariat. Here is what the programme said on this point:

whereas the deprivation of political freedom is an obstacle on the way towards the social education of the people and the economic emancipation of the proletariat;

. . . considering also that political activity is useful as an agitational means and that the election arena is doubtless an arena for struggle from which one should not flee, the Congress *confirms* the decisions adopted on this question by the socialist, national and international congresses and declares:

(1) That the social emancipation of the workers is inseparably linked up with their political emancipation;

(2) That to abstain from political activity would yield disastrous results;

(3) That while revolution is the sole means of liberating the working class, this revolution is possible only with and by means of an organised working class.

Further, of course, there follow the political and economic programmes, which contain the demand for the abolition of all political obstacles to the development of the labour movement, demands connected with working hours, wages, the abolition of indirect taxes, etc. It must be noted that this programme was on a higher level than the Gotha programme of German Social-Democracy in 1875. However, also in this programme, not everything was as it should have been. In his letter to Bernstein, dated October 25, 1881, Engels wrote:

Guesde insisted on including his rubbish about *Minimum du Salaire* (minimum wage), and, in view of the fact that it was not we but the French who were responsible for this, we finally gave in to him, although he (Marx) admitted the theoretical absurdity of this.[1]

The Workers' Party, created with the direct political and organisational help of Marx and Engels, came to be the arena for fierce struggles between the Marxists and the Possibilists, the leader of whom was Benoit Malon. The struggle was carried on in connection with very important problems of principle: parliamentary socialism or revolutionary socialism, class collaboration or class struggle. On the other hand, the Blanquists, headed by Vaillant, set up their own party, and finally anti-

[1] Marx and Engels, *Selected Works.*

Marxist views strengthened in the trade unions where the Proud-honist-Bakuninist ideas were quite widespread.

Marx systematically followed the work of Guesde, Lafargue and the Workers' Party. He utilised his trip to Paris at the beginning of 1882 to familiarise himself thoroughly with the internal life of the socialist and trade union movement of France. Marx, in a number of letters to Engels, expressed his views on the policy and tactics of Guesde and Lafargue, the leaders of the Workers' Party. Marx, who highly esteemed Lafargue and Guesde, sharply criticised his son-in-law Lafargue for his desire to outyell the anarchists; he stated that in one of his articles he, Lafargue, had called Fourier a Communist and didn't know how to get out of it, that he occupied himself with "childish boasting of the terrible deeds he would perform in the coming revolution," that he, Lafargue, "goes too far in his prophecies," etc. Marx was particularly dissatisfied with the manner in which Lafargue attempted to struggle against Bakunin while at the same time adopting his platform. "Longet —last of the Proudhonists; Lafargue—last of the Bakuninists, 'To the devil with them!' " [1] Marx exclaimed in his letter to Engels dated November 11, 1882. The state of the French socialist and trade union organisations disturbed Marx all along.

> Concerning the Paris "syndicates" [Marx wrote to Engels on November 27, 1882], I know by questioning impartial Parisians during my stay that these syndicates are, perhaps, much worse than the London Trade Unions. [2]

The struggle in the Workers' Party between the Marxists and anti-Marxists grew to be more and more acute. Malon and Brousse headed all the opportunist elements, and at the congress of the Workers' Party in 1882 the whole of the Marxist wing was expelled. This split came not unexpectedly for Marx and Engels. On October 28, 1882, Engels wrote to Bebel:

> The long-expected split has occurred in France. The initial collaboration of Guesde and Lafargue with Malon and Brousse

[1] Marx and Engels, *Complete Works* (German edition), Part III, Vol. 4, pp. 524–25.
[2] *Ibid.*, p. 569.

could not very well be avoided when the Party was organised; however, Marx and I never had any illusion about the lasting nature of this alliance. The difference is purely one of principle; ought the struggle to be waged as a class struggle of the proletariat against the bourgeoisie, or is it to be permissible in good opportunist fashion (or translated into socialist language, in good Possibilist fashion) to drop the class character of the movement and the programme wherever by so doing it is possible to get more votes, more adherents? Malon and Brousee came out for the latter; thus they sacrificed the proletarian class character of the movement and rendered the split inevitable. Very well, then. *The development of the proletariat is everywhere the result of internal struggles,* and France, where a workers' party is organised for the first time, is no exception.[1]

Benoit Malon made advances to the trade unions, trying to get them to form a *bloc* against the Marxists. On November 23, 1882, Engels wrote to Marx:

Evidently it was precisely in order to please the trade unions that Malon and Co. sacrificed the programme and the whole past of the movement since the time of the Marseilles Congress. What appears to be his power is in reality his weakness. If one lowers one's programme to the level of the most ordinary trade unions, it is easy indeed to have a 'big public.' [2]

Thus, in 1882, a Marxist Party appeared in France. When one familiarises oneself with the activities of French Marxism from 1882 to 1914, the impression one gets is not very cheering. Guesde doubtless was for some time a revolutionary, but Guesde's Marxism was always of a nationalist character. Marx and Engels were frequently quoted, but Marxism in France did not develop into a great force, although the Workers' Party did have a number of deputies in Parliament and some influence over the masses. French Marxism went from one extreme to the other. Guesde was doubtless the best Marxist in France; however, his Marxism did not always come from Marx: Guesde's Marxism always contained much that was added by himself. This was excellently proved during the World War, when French Marxism, in the person of Guesde, Bracke, etc., sancti-

[1] Archives 1 (VI), Marx-Engels-Lenin Institute, Mocow.
[2] Marx and Engels, *Complete Works* (German edition), Part III, Vol. 4, pp. 574--75.

fied the plunderers' war as the final war, as the struggle of democracy against militarism. Thus there was something corrupt about French Marxism, since it could not pass this historic test. True, all socialist, anarchist and anarcho-syndicalist grouping went bankrupt in 1914, but this in no way lessens the significance of the fact that the only Marxian organisation in France at that time went hand in hand with the bitterest enemies of the working class in the defence of the interests of French imperialism. How can this be explained? By the fact that French Marxism, just like all socialist and anarchist tendencies of France, suffered from *exceptionalism*. The French socialists considered themselves inheritors of the "Great Revolution" and always believed France to be the centre of the earth. French Marxism, parallel with the growth of French imperialism, came to be more and more national, *i.e.*, stopped being Marxism. This castration of Marxism deprives it of its revolutionary spirit, and it occurred also in Germany, under the influence of these same causes, against which both Marx and Engels had given warnings long before the World War. The French and German Marxists went bankrupt, on the same day they slipped on one and the same patriotic peel; French Marxism became national, and *wherever the national elbows out the class, there can be no more Marxism.*

Did the war lead to the bankruptcy of Marxism? No. The war exposed all the rottenness that had penetrated the Marxist parties, it showed that nationalist propaganda had been carried on under the banner of Marxism. It is not Marxism that went bankrupt, but pseudo-Marxism, which came out openly in all countries as the lackey of the imperialist bourgeoisie. While pseudo-Marxism and all anti-Marxian groupings were smashed, the Party which observed the traditions of Marx, and the Party which brought up its cadres on a revolutionary Marxist footing, the Party of Lenin, actually showed what revolutionary Marxism is. History does not develop along straight lines, it has its high and low tides, its ups and downs, its intermissions, and its stormy whirlwind ascents. Through the crash of official Marxism and anarcho-syndicalism the French proletariat came to the point of creating a real party of revolutionary Marxism. This Party grew up and developed in the struggle against the betrayal of Marxism by the inheritors of Marx; it grew out of the revolutionary rejection of all corruption observed in pre-war French Marxism, it grew up in the struggle against the inheritors of Proudhon, Malon, Brousse, Jaurès and Guesde; in the struggle against false French democracy, which cunningly screened its imperialist lust with revolutionary-historical mysticism. The Communist Party of France is the only bearer of the revolutionary teachings of Marx, for outside the Communist Party there is not and cannot be any revolutionary Marxism.

CHAPTER VI

Marx and the United States

If we were minded to build up an ideal country for capitalist development, basing ourselves upon the environment of a capitalist economic system, that country would in no wise differ from the United States in its special features and dimensions.[1]

THIS is how Werner Sombart characterises this promised land of monopolist capitalism. During the period when Marx appeared on the political arena, the United States swallowed up tremendous masses of emigrants from Europe. The powerful immigration torrent was rapidly absorbed in this gigantic country, but it did not subside, it constantly grew, attracting ever new nationalities and social strata: artisans ruined by the introduction of the machine, unemployed who had been forced out of the infant industries, and proletarianised peasants, as well as numerous elements from the urban petty-bourgeoisie. Emigration reached enormous proportions after the defeat of the revolution in Germany, Austria and France in 1848. Thus, from 1790 to 1845, 1,000,000 persons settled in the United States, while from 1845 to 1855, 3,000,000; the overwhelming majority of settlers, however, went to the United States after 1848.[2] This unceasing structure of American economics—pure capitalism, based on "free" labour in the North and slavery in the South—laid a special imprint on the labour movement in the United States.

Marx in his *The Eighteenth Brumaire* characterises the specific situation and the undeveloped class relationships in the

[1] Werner Sombart, *Outline of History of Development of the North American Proletariat.*

[2] A. Bimba, *History of the American Labour Movement* (1930).

United States during the first half of the nineteenth century:

> The country where the classes already constituted but not yet fixed modify and constantly replace, on the other hand, their constituent elements; where the modern means of production, instead of corresponding to a stagnant overpopulation, compensate rather for the relative lack of heads and arms; and where, finally, the young movement throbs with material production which has a new world to conquer, has had neither time nor occasion for destroying the ancient spiritual world.[1]

These undifferentiated class relationships were a favourable ground for those who were "seeking to attain the emancipation of the proletariat, so to speak, behind the back of society, privately, within the restricted bounds of its conditions of existence." [2]

Vast territories of virgin soil attracted the attention of European utopians, who hoped to organise their communities on the promised land. In 1824 Robert Owen himself went to the United States, bought a considerable tract of land and began to organise ideal societies, where the workers and the capitalists, who recanted past sins and greed, were expected to live peacefully side by side and help one another. With the aid of philanthropists he organised the Yellow Spring Community in 1825, then the "New Harmony," the "Nashoba," "Kendel" and other communities.

During the first half of the nineteenth century Fourier societies sprang up in the states of Massachusetts, New York, New Jersey, Pennsylvania, Ohio, Illinois, Indiana, Wisconsin and Minnesota. The organisers of these communities—Albert Brisbane, Horace Greeley, and others, built special phalanxes according to the Fourier plan; however, just as in the case of the communities built by the adherents of Robert Owen, nothing came of it. The best of the communities, as, for example, the *North-American* phalanx known as Brook Farm, the Wisconsin phalanx, the Pennsylvania group, the New York group and others, merely vegetated and finally disintegrated. The same was

---

[1] *The Eighteenth Brumaire of Louis Bonaparte* (French edition), Paris, 1928, p. 33.
[2] *Ibid.,* p. 32.

the fate of the Icarian Communities, organised by followers of the utopian Communist Etienne Cabet.[1] The United States proved to be a promised land for capitalism and a harsh land for all the noble social experiments of utopian socialism.

Who were the initiators and pioneers of the building of socialist communities on American soil, so free and clear of all feudalism? The European adherents of the utopian socialists who had become disappointed in revolutions and were in search of ways for solving the social problem outside the class struggle. Marx highly valued the utopian socialists, not for their utopianism but for their socialism. He considered them forerunners of critico-materialist socialism. But Marx was merciless towards the utopian communists of the type of Weitling who attempted to resurrect utopian socialism some dozens of years after it had been buried. Weitling, who at first had followed Marx, began to call himself a prophet and the founder of a special school. The chief work of Weitling, *The Guaranties of Harmony and Freedom,* was a sentimental communist appeal not to live as of old but to begin a new life. After arriving in the United States in the 'forties, he began to do organisational work, chiefly among German immigrants, and to set himself and his teaching up against Marx and Marxism. The years 1850-60 saw Weitling's activities at their peak. He succeeded in rallying considerable sections of the German workers around him; however, his endeavour to create his own school and his confused philosophy led not only to his breaking with Marx, but also with workers who had followed him for several years. Marx, in his letter to Sorge, dated October 19, 1877, characterised Weitling's utopian socialism and utopian communism in the following way:

> That of which we have swept clean the heads of the workers for decades with so much labour and effort, and which gave them the theoretical (and consequently also the practical) preponderance over the French and the British—*utopian socialism, the play of fancy in the realm of the future structure of society—is rampant again in much inferior form* [Italics mine.—*A.L.*], not to be compared with the great French and British utopians but with Weitling. It is natural that utopianism, which pre-

[1] Morris Hillquit, *History of Socialism in the United States,* Funk & Wagnalls, 1906.

maturely harboured materialist-critical socialism (in embryo) can now, when it arrives *post festum* [after its time.—ED.] be only silly, tiresome, and at bottom reactionary.[1]

We see how Marx establishes the relationship between scientific socialism and utopian socialism, and how severely he criticises those who to their old age flaunt about in the children's clothes of utopian socialism, who try to drag back the labour movement in the United States.

The main stream of emigrants came from Germany, and therefore socialism was imported from there, but during the early years it could not take firm root on American soil because pre-Marxian German socialism had been rather helpless on German soil, and with its transplantation to American soil became weaker still. The immigrants brought along from Europe not only utopian ideas, but also the European forms of organisation of that period. The structure of the working class in the United States was very peculiar and variegated at that time and has remained so till now. This made it more difficult to bring socialist ideas to the masses. Two factors played a decisive *rôle* in forming the ideology of the working class of that period— slavery and immigration. In his first volume of *Capital* Marx writes:

> In the United States of North America every independent movement of the workers was paralysed so long as slavery disfigured a part of the Republic. Labour cannot emancipate itself in the white skin where in the black it is branded.[1]

If we add to this black brand the masses of immigrants who were ready to work for a pittance, if only to earn a crust of bread, we see wherein lay the cause for the special state of the labour movement in the United States at that time. Immigration fixed its special imprint on the working class of the United States, creating various strata and groups in the midst of the working class, according to nationality, degree of knowledge of the English language, etc. In 1893 Engels wrote to Sorge:

[1] Marx, *Letters to Sorge,* 1907.
[2] *Capital,* Vol. I, p. 329, Kerr edition.

. . . immigration . . . divides the workers into two groups—native- and foreign-born, and the latter into: (1) Irish, (2) German, and (3) many small groups, the members of each of which can only understand one another, namely, Czechs, Poles, Italians, Scandinavians, etc. And then we must add the Negroes. Particularly favourable conditions are needed to form a single party out of this. Sometimes there is a powerful élan; however, the bourgeoisie need merely hold out passively for the heterogeneous elements of the working masses to fall apart again.[1]

In 1895 Engels returned again to the question of the specific traits of the labour movement in the United States, where tremendously intensive economic battles had occurred during the nineteenth century, while the political movement of the proletariat developed in an extremely zig-zag manner, never reaching a high peak of exceptional sharpness or intensity. This resulted in the ideological-political lagging behind of the labour movement in the United States. How does Engels explain this lagging behind? In his letter to Sorge of January 16, 1895, Engels wrote:

America is the *youngest but also the oldest country in the world*. Just as you in your country have ancient Frankonian furniture alongside of that which you have yourselves invented, just as in Boston there are carriages such as I saw for the last time in London in 1838; and in the mountains you have stage-coaches dating back to the seventeenth century, alongside of Pullman cars; so, in the same way, you preserve *all old discarded spiritual costumes of Europe. All that has gone out of existence here can continue to live in America for two generations more.* [Italics mine.—A.L.] Thus in your country the old Lassalleans continue to exist, while people of the type of Sanial, who would to-day be considered antiquated in France, can still play some part in your country. This is due on the one hand to the fact that in America after worrying about material production and acquisition of wealth, they only now have time for independent spiritual activities and the requisite education; on the other hand, because of the dual character of America's development, which, for one thing, is still working on the first task—clearing off the vast virgin territories, and, for another, is already compelled to compete for supremacy in industrial production.

[1] *Letters to Sorge*, 1907.

This is what causes the ups and downs in the movement, depending upon whether the industrial worker or the farmer tilling virgin soil preponderates in the average mind.[1]

This letter of Engels explains the singularity of the labour movement in the United States, particularly during the epoch of Marx.

Contact between the American workers and communism, also with its famous founder, Marx, was first established by the worker-immigrants from Germany.

The earliest German forerunner of Marx—writes John R. Commons, historian of the labour movement in the United States—was the Communist Club in New York, a Marxian organisation, based on the *Communist Manifesto,* established on October 25, 1857. The programme of the club was the *Communist Manifesto.* The membership was not large, but it comprised many who subsequently made themselves prominent in the American International, such as F. A. Sorge, Conrad Carl, Siegfried Meyer, etc. The club kept up connections with the communist movement abroad, and among its correspondents we find men like Karl Marx, Johann Philip Becker of Geneva, Joseph Weydemeyer. . . . [2]

Simultaneously with the organisation of Marxist clubs in the United States, various Lassallean organisations also sprang up, of which the largest was the General Union of German Workers, founded in New York in October 1865 by fourteen Lassalle adherents. They brought from the other side of the ocean their confused ideas, which can be seen from the following clause in their statutes:

While in Europe only a general revolution can form the means of uplifting the working people, in America the education of the masses will instil into them the degree of self-confidence as is indispensable to the effective and intelligent use of the ballot and will eventually lead to the emancipation of the working people from the yoke of capitalism.[3]

---

[1] *Ibid.*
[2] J. R. Commons, *History of the Labour Movement in the United States,* Vol. II., Macmillan, 1921.
[3] *Ibid.*

In all the main cities of the United States workers' clubs, unions and all kinds of societies were organised; these tried to set up contacts with the spiritual-political centre of that time— with London, where Marx and Engels lived. The emigrant organisations thoroughly studied Marxist literature, primarily the works of Marx himself. Sorge vividly describes how the German workers followed up Marxian literature and studied it carefully. Sorge wrote:

> These proletarians . . . compete with one another in acquiring economic and philosophical problems. Among the hundreds of members who belonged to the society from 1869 to 1874 there was barely anyone who had not read his Marx (*Capital*) and there were, of course, more than a dozen of them who had assimilated and mastered the most difficult phrases and definitions, and were thus equipped against any attacks by the big bourgeoisie or petty bourgeois, by radicals or reformers. It was indeed a pleasure to attend meetings of the society.[1]

Simultaneously with the growth and development of immigrant, chiefly German, unions, clubs, groups, etc., the 'fifties and 'sixties of the nineteenth century can be characterised also by the growth of the trade unions, the sharpening of the struggle for shorter working hours, for labour legislation, for the protection of female and child labour, etc. A number of local and international trade union organisations sprang up—of metal workers, miners, founders, shipbuilding workers, etc. The trade union leaders of that time conceived the idea of establishing a national labour union. The initiator and organiser of this union was William H. Sylvis, the moulder, first secretary and afterwards president of the International Moulders' Union. The International Engineers' and Blacksmiths' Union already in 1863 advanced the idea of creating a national trade union organisation. In 1864 the International Moulders' Union also supported this idea. On March 26, 1866, the officials of a number of unions in various cities arrived in New York and issued an appeal to convene a National Labour Congress in Baltimore on August 20, 1868. The aims of the Congress were defined by its initiators in the following way:

[1] F. Sorge, *Labour Movement in the United States*, 1907.

The first and greatest need of the present, if labour in this country is to be liberated from capitalist slavery, is the passing of a *law* which will provide that eight hours shall constitute a normal working day in *all* the states of the Union. We are determined to do everything in our power to attain this result.

The decision adopted at the Labour Congress in Baltimore was joyfully welcomed by Marx. In his letter to Kugelmann dated October 9, 1866, Marx wrote:

I was very pleased with the American Workers' Congress at Baltimore [which was convened simultaneously with the Geneva Congress of the International Workingmen's Association.—*A.L.*]. The slogan there was organisation for the struggle against capital, and curiously enough most of the demands which I drew up for Geneva were also put forward by the correct instinct of the workers.[1]

It is not surprising that the demands drawn up by Marx for the Geneva Congress (see chapter on Partial Demands) coincided with the demands of the advanced workers in the United States. Marx knew the international labour movement better than any one else, and the programme of demands worked out by him was a generalisation of the demands of the workers in all capitalist countries and was based on the experiences acquired in the class struggle and the communist attitude towards the "true instinct of the workers."

Two years later Marx again referred to this Congress; in his letter to Kugelmann, dated December 12, 1868, he wrote:

Joking aside, great progress was evident in the last Congress of the American 'Labour Union' in that, among other things, it treated working women with complete equality. While in this respect the English, and still more the gallant French, are burdened with a spirit of narrow-mindedness. Anybody who knows anything of history knows that great social changes are impossible without the feminine ferment. Social progress can be measured exactly by the social position of the fair sex (the ugly ones included).

---

[1] Marx, *Letters to Kugelmann*, p. 83.

This letter once again proves that Marx knew just what he wanted in all problems of social movements, excellently bearing in mind that limiting the rights of women workers in working-class organisations means political self-limitation of the working class.

This Congress, which adopted a decision on the struggle for the eight-hour working day, was noted by Marx in his first volume of *Capital*, where he emphasised that:

> Out of the death of slavery a new life at once arose. The first fruit of the Civil War was the eight-hours' agitation, that ran with the seven-league boots of the locomotive from the Atlantic to the Pacific, from New England to California.[1]

This National Labour Union, the initiator and organiser of which was William Sylvis, held a number of other congresses (in 1867, 1868, 1869, 1870 and 1871). It set up contacts with the International Workingmen's Association, and although the best leaders of that time, as for example Sylvis, were not particularly firm on questions of socialist programmes and tactics, Marx followed this movement very attentively and highly esteemed its militant activity for shorter working hours, for higher wages, etc.

In connection with the strained relations between England and the United States in 1869, the General Council issued an appeal to the National Labour Union in which it called on the working class of the United States to fight determinedly against war, which brings nothing to the working class of Europe and America but disaster. This appeal written by Marx is so characteristic of the whole position of the First International and Marx himself, that we give here quite substantial quotations from it:

> In the inaugural programme of our Association we stated: "It was not the wisdom of the ruling classes, but the heroic resistance to their criminal folly by the working class of England that saved the West of Europe from plunging headlong into an infamous crusade for the perpetuation and propagation of slavery on the other side of the Atlantic." Your turn has now come to stop a war, the clearest result of which would be for an indefinite period

[1] *Capital*, Vol. I, p. 329, Kerr edition.

to hurl back the ascendent movement of the working class on both sides of the Atlantic. . . .

Quite apart from the particular interests of this or that government, is it not the general interest of our common oppressors to turn our fast-growing international co-operation into an internecine war? . . . In our address to Mr. Lincoln, on his re-election as President, we expressed our conviction that the American Civil War would prove of as great importance to the advancement of the working class, as the American War of Independence had proved to that of the middle class. And, in point of fact, the victorious termination of the anti-slavery war has opened a new epoch in the annals of the working class. In the United States an independent working-class movement, looked upon with a jealous eye by your old parties and their professional politicians, has since that date sprung into being. It requires years of peace before this movement will bear fruit. To crush it a war between the United States and England is needed.

The aggravation of the position of the American worker was certainly the immediate and tangible result of the Civil War. Moreover, the sufferings of the working class are set off by the insolent luxury of financial aristocracy, shoddy aristocrats and similar vermin bred by war like parasites. Yet, for all this, the Civil War did compensate by freeing the slaves and the consequent moral impetus it gave to our own class movement. A second war, not hallowed by a sublime purpose and a great social necessity, but a war after the fashion of the Old World would only forge chains for the worker, instead of tearing asunder those of the slave. The aggravation of the misery left in its track would afford your capitalists at once the motive and means to divorce the working class from its bold and just aspirations by the soulless sword of a standing army.

On you then depends the glorious task to prove to the world that now at last the working classes are bestriding the scene of history no longer as the servile retainers but as independent factors conscious of their own responsibility and able to command peace where their would-be masters shout war.[1]

---

[1] This appeal was signed by the following, on behalf of the General Council of the International Workingmen's Association:

British Nation: R. Applegarth, carpenter; M. J. Boon, engineer; J. Backley, painter; J. Hales, weaver; Harriet Law; B. Lucraft, chairmaker; D. Milner, tailor; Odger, shoemaker; J. Ross, bootcloser; B. Shaw, painter; Cowell Stepney; J. Warren, trunkmaker; J. Weston, hand-rail maker.

French Nation: Dupont, instrument maker; Jules Johannard, lithographer; Paul Lafargue.

G

This appeal raises a number of very important problems, first and foremost the problem of the attitude of the working-class organisations generally *and the Trade Unions in particular, towards war.* Marx does not come out against war "generally," but puts the question concretely. He emphasises the good sides of the Civil War for the workers and the disadvantages of the impending Anglo-American war. This appeal did not remain without a reply from the President of the National Labour Union, Sylvis. In his report to the Basle Congress Marx wrote:

> The sudden death of Mr. Sylvis, that valiant champion of our cause, will justify us in concluding this report by appending his reply to our letter as a homage to his memory:
> "Your favour of the 12th instant, with address enclosed, reached me yesterday. I am very happy to receive such kindly words from our fellow-working men across the water; our cause is a common one. It is war between poverty and wealth: labour occupies the same low condition and capital is the same tyrant in all parts of the world. Therefore, I say our cause is a common one. I, on behalf of the working people of the United States, extend to you and through you to those you represent and to all the down-trodden and oppressed sons and daughters of toil in Europe, the right hand of fellowship. Go ahead in the good work you have undertaken, until the most glorious success crowns your efforts. This is our determination. Our late war resulted in the building up of the most infamous monied aristocracy on the face of the earth. This monied power is fast eating up the substance of the people. We have made war upon it and we mean to win. If we can, we will win through the ballot box; if not, then we will resort to sterner means. A little blood-letting is something necessary in desperate cases." [1]

This letter is very characteristic of the leader of the young

German Nation: D. Eccarius, tailor; F. Lessner, tailor; W. Limburg, shoe-maker; Karl Marx.
Swedish Nation: H. Jung, watchmaker; A. Muller, watchmaker.
Belgian Nation: P. Bernard, painter.
Danish Nation: D. Cohn, cigar-maker.
Polish Nation: Zabicky, compositor.
E. Lucraft, chairman; Cowell Stepney, treasurer; George Eccarius, General Secretary.

Quotations taken from text at Marx-Engels-Lenin Institute.—*Ed.*
[1] *Report of the General Council to Basle Congress,* Archives, M.-E.-L.-I.

American trade union movement and shows that it was no accident when Marx in his report called Sylvis a "valiant fighter."

From the minutes of the General Council of the International Workingmen's Association it can be seen that problems concerning the American labour movement were repeatedly placed on the agenda. Thus, in the minutes of the General Council of April 8, 1869, we read:

A letter was read from the newspaper printers of New York in which they request the Council to exercise its influence in order to prevent the import of labour power, which aims at defeating the workers who are now out on strike. The secretary was charged with writing to all newspapers abroad controlled by the International Workingmen's Association.

At the same meeting of the General Council a report was made by a committee on the question of the immigration bureau, and the following decision was adopted:

(1) The immigration bureau was established in co-operation with the National Labour Union.
(2) In case of strikes the Council will have to strain all efforts to prevent the American employers from recruiting workers in Europe.[1]

Again, just as it had done with regard to the British trade unions, the General Council, under the leadership of Marx, raised questions of the economic struggle (struggle against strike-breakers, etc.) for the purpose of setting up strong contacts with the trade unions in the United States. This is borne out by the minutes of April 19, 1870, in which we read:

A letter is read from Hume, New York correspondent, who pointed out that the trade union movement tended to assume the form of secret societies in the United States. This was confirmed by a letter from the German correspondents in New York, who appealed to the Council to interfere by trying to dissuade Hume and Jessup from taking part in it. It was agreed that the Council, under present circumstances, was not in a position to

[1] Minutes of General Council of I.W.A.

decide upon the merits of this question. The secretary should write and ask what was the cause that necessitated secret societies in America.[1]

The communication from New York and the decision of the General Council show that Marx and the International Workingmen's Association went into all details of the movement, and in those cases when they did not adopt immediate decisions, they collected necessary information and maintained permanent contacts with their section and adherents. These permanent contacts and this political aid to the movement can especially be seen from the correspondence of Marx and Engels with Sorge and others during that period, when sections of the International Workingmen's Association began to spring up in New York and many other cities and political and organisational differences arose in the ranks of these sections.

Marx, in his letter to Sorge dated September 1, 1870, writes about the distribution of functions in the General Council, and that the secretary for the United States should be Eccarius; on September 21, 1871, Marx advised Sorge to call the newly-elected leading body "Central Committee" instead of "Central Council," and to let him know what literature had been forwarded to America; on September 12, 1871, Marx wrote to Sorge about the circulars and the statutes of the International Workingmen's Association sent to him. On November 6, 1871, Marx again wrote about pamphlets, literature and the famous Section 12 in New York, which was composed of journalists and intellectuals who aspired to take over the leadership of the movement. On November 9, Marx advised Sorge to convene a congress after preliminary organisational and political work, and to set up a federal committee; he tried to persuade Sorge not to leave the committee; on November 10, 1871, Marx wrote to Speyer, one of the members of the Central Committee:

(1) According to the statutes, the General Council in the land of the Yankees had first of all to keep its eyes on the Yankees....
(2) You must try at all costs to win over the trade unions.[2]

[1] Minutes of the General Council of the International Workingmen's Association, Archives, Marx-Engels-Lenin Institute.
[2] Letters from Becker, Dietzgen, Engels and Marx, etc. to Sorge and others, p. 38.

In this letter Marx replies in detail to a number of reproaches and suspicions in regard to the General Council, trying to convince his correspondent that the General Council will not be able to forbid its members to carry on private correspondence; on November 23, Marx in a letter to Bolte explained why the International Workingmen's Association was compelled "in the beginning to entrust powers to private persons in the United States and to make them its correspondents."

In the same letter to Bolte Marx wrote:

> The International was formed for the purpose of putting the real organisation of the working class for the struggle in the place of the socialist and semi-socialist sects. The original rules as well as the *Inaugural Address* show this at first glance. On the other hand the adherents of the International could not have maintained their position if the course of history had not already had sectarianism. The development of socialist sectarianism and that of the real labour movement are constantly in inverse proportion to each other. As long as sects are justified (historically), the working class is not yet sufficiently mature for an independent historical movement. As soon as it reaches this degree of maturity, all sects are essentially reactionary. Meanwhile the history of the adherents of the International repeated what history everywhere shows. The obsolete seeks to renovate and maintain itself within the newly won forms.[1]

This remarkable passage in Marx's letter explains his tactics with regard to the trade unions, with regard to the different socialist and semi-socialist organisations, the principles underlying his attitude towards sectarianism and his methods of struggle for a correct communist policy.

At the same time a struggle flared up among the adherents of the International Workingmen's Association in the U.S.A. This struggle found its expression in the appeal which the Federal Council, consisting of a few dozen sections and Section 12 of New York, sent to the General Council in London, requesting it to settle their dispute. The General Council, under the leadership of Marx, came out against Section 12, in which petty-bourgeois politicians tried to domineer, and backed the

[1] *Ibid.*

Federal Council, around which the workers were grouped. On March 8, 1872, Marx wrote to Sorge:

> As the General Council instructed me to make a report on the split in America (owing to the conflicts in the ranks of the European sections of the International, the matter had to be postponed from meeting to meeting), I carefully examined all of the correspondence from New York and everything published in the newspapers on the subject, and came to the conclusion that we had not at all been informed in time as to the elements which caused the rupture. The part of the resolution which I proposed has already been adopted; the rest will be passed next Tuesday, after which the final decision will be forwarded to New York.[1]

On March 15, 1872, Marx sent to Sorge a copy of the resolution, which he had drafted and which had been adopted by the General Council. As this resolution splendidly characterises both Marx and the International Workingmen's Association, we quote it in full:

> (1) Both councils shall combine to form one provisional Federal Council;
> (1a) New and small sections shall combine in sending delegates;
> (2) A general congress of the American members of the International must be convened on July 1;
> (2a) This congress shall elect a Federal Council authorised to co-opt members;
> (2b) and also work out the rules and statutes of the Federal Council;
> (3) Section 12 (in view of its pretensions and quackery) shall be suspended until the next general congress;
> (3a) At least two-thirds of every section must consist of wage workers.[2]

The Hague Congress of the First International resolved to transfer the headquarters of the International Workingmen's Association to the U.S.A. The attack of the Bakuninists had thus been warded off; however, this marked the beginning of the end of the First International as an international working-class organisation. But whilst this signified a backward step for

---

[1] *Letters to Sorge*, 1907.
[2] *Ibid.* See Note I to letter of Marx to Sorge, March 15, 1872.

Europe, for the United States it acted as an impetus to rally all
Marxian elements around the General Council. On the other
hand, the enemies of Marxism also closed their ranks. Marx
and Engels knew that the New York General Council, the International Workingmen's Association and the London General
Council were not the same by far. They did everything in their
power politically and organisationally to support the General
Council; however, the struggle around it sharpened and splits
occurred. Thanks to Sorge and others the General Council tried
to act in the spirit of Marx and Engels. But one of the weakest
spots was the attitude of the sections of the International towards
the trade unions. On June 3, 1874, the General Council sent the
following letter to Section 3 in Chicago:

> It appears strange that we should have to point out to a section
> of the International the usefulness and extraordinary importance
> of the trade union movement. Nevertheless, we shall remind
> Section 3 that each of the congresses of the I.W.A., from the first
> to the last, diligently occupied itself with the trade union move-
> ment and sought to devise means of furthering it. The trade
> union is the cradle of the labour movement, for working people
> naturally turn first to that which affects their daily life, and they
> consequently combine first with their fellows by trade. It there-
> fore becomes the duty of the members of the International not
> merely to assist the existing trade unions, and, before all, to lead
> them to the right path, *i.e.*, to internationalise them, but also to
> establish new ones wherever possible. The economic conditions
> are driving the trade unions with irresistible force from the
> economic to the political struggle, against the propertied classes—
> a truth which is known to all those who observe the labour move-
> ment with open eyes.[1]

This real Marxist policy, correct in principle, was, however,
crossed by all sorts of other influences and the American General
Council began to slip more and more from the Marxist position.

In 1876 the last of the Mohicans who supported the General
Council were forced to dissolve the International Workingmen's
Association. Thus, the International Workingmen's Association,
this political and organisational creation of Marx, went out of

[1] Commons, *History of Labour in the U.S.A.*, Vol. II, p. 229 (Macmillan,
1921).

existence—the international labour movement made a new sharp turn.

Karl Marx followed the various phases of the labour movement in the United States more closely than anyone else. He saw its specific traits, its various dark sides and difficulties. What, then, were the instructions that Marx gave to his adherents in the United States? Marx called upon them to pay maximum attention to the trade unions, to merge with the working class and to eradicate all "narrow, moss-grown sectarian tendencies out of the organisations." Marx demanded amalgamation with the mass movement, seeing in this the best guarantee against sectarianism and opportunism; however, his demands were not fulfilled. The Labour and trade union movement in the U.S.A. travelled along a special path; the flourishing of American capitalism meant the simultaneous bourgeoisification of American trade unionism. Its theoretician and leader for many years, Samuel Gompers, was the enemy of socialism, a mere politician and money-maker. Marxism for many years was driven back by Gompersism, by the policy and practice of imperialist corruption and demoralisation. The trade unions began to be headed by outright business men, whose slogan was—not a labour policy, but a businesslike, capitalist policy.

In order to characterise reactionary trade unionism, let us quote some of the evidence given in 1883 (the year of Marx's death) to the Senate Commission by Strasser, President of the International Cigar-Makers' Union, of which Gompers was secretary:

QUESTION: You are seeking to improve home matters first?
ANSWER: Yes, sir, I look first to the trade I represent; I look first to cigars, to the interests of men who employ me to represent their interests.
QUESTION: I was only asking you in regard to your ultimate aims.
ANSWER: We have no ultimate aims. We are going on from day to day. We are fighting, only for immediate objects, objects that can be realised in a few years.
QUESTION: You want something better to eat and to wear and better houses to live in?
ANSWER: Yes, we want to dress better, and to live better, and to become better citizens, generally.

CHAIRMAN OF COMMISSION: I see that you are a little sensitive lest it should be thought that you are a mere theoriser. I do not look upon you in that light.

WITNESS: Well, we say in our constitution that we are opposed to theorists and I have to represent the organisation here. We are all practical men.[1]

What Strasser left unsaid was said by Gompers, by John Mitchel, author of *Organised Labour,* and all others who in theory and practice betrayed the interests of the working class, who brought to a logical conclusion their policy of ideologically, politically and organisationally subordinating the trade unions to the trusts.

What are the reasons for the historically temporary setback given to Marxism by Gompersism? The basic cause was the victorious progressive development of American capitalism which in consequence enabled the bourgeoisie to bribe and corrupt some sections of the better-paid workers, whilst the standard of living of the majority of the working class, diverse in its composition, remained below minimum.

It seems to us that of late, servile, reactionary Gompersism is visibly rolling down the slope together with capitalism. The Marxian spirit can be sensed in demonstrations, in bloody strikes and hunger marches of the unemployed in the U.S.A. Revolutionary Marxism is winning one position after another.

The American bourgeoisie is unable to check the process of disintegration of its national economy, and to a still smaller degree are the hirelings of the trusts, the trade union inheritors of Gompers, able to do so. Who, then, has proved to be historically right? In whose favour is history working? Evidently in favour of revolutionary Marxism and not Gompersism.

[1] S. Perelman, *History of Trade Unionism in the United States,* 1923, p. 79.

CHAPTER VII

Marx and the Struggle for the Partial Demands of the Working Class

Is there any sense in fighting for shorter hours, higher wages, etc? For scores of years this was the theoretical and political question that occupied the centre of the scientific and political struggle of Marx. To put the question this way would to-day seem very strange to us and even unworthy of any attention, but this is so because Marx accomplished tremendous scientific and political tasks in this direction. We have seen that Marx fought against Proudhon, Lassalle, and Weston, *i.e.,* against the most distinguished representatives of French, German and English petty-bourgeois socialism, on the question of the usefulness of trade unions and strikes, on the question of what are wages, price and profit, etc. Proudhon, Lassalle and Weston took their theories from the British bourgeois economists, who proved in the name of science and God that the struggle of the trade unions to improve the conditions of the workers is at best futile, not to mention the fact that it violates every law of God and man.

In the first volume of *Capital,* Marx collected a rich bouquet of anti-labour arguments, decorated with high-sounding scientific phrases advanced by Adam Smith, John Stuart Mill, McCulloch, Ure, Bastiat, Sue, James, Stirling, Cairnes, Walker, etc. In order to show the extent to which these "scientific" arguments were imbued with the employers' spirit, let me give a few quotations here:

> All the capital through the haggling of the market will be equitably distributed among all labourers. Hence it is idle to suppose that the efforts of the capitalists to cheapen labour can have the smallest influence on its medium price. (McCulloch.)

There is supposed to be at any given instant a sum of wealth which is unconditionally devoted to the payment of wages of labour. This sum is not regarded as unalterable, for it is augmented by saving and increases with the progress of society; but it is reasoned upon as at any given moment a predetermined amount. More than that amount it is assumed that the wage-receiving class cannot possibly divide among them; that amount and no less they cannot but obtain. So that the sum to be divided being fixed, the wages of each depend solely on the divisor, the number of participants. (John Stuart Mill.)

That which pays for labour in every country is a certain portion of actually accumulated capital, which cannot be increased by conscious intervention of government, nor by the influence of public opinion, nor by combinations among workmen themselves. There is also in every country a certain number of labourers, and this number cannot be diminished by the proposed action of government nor by public opinion, nor by combinations among themselves. There is to be a division now among all these labourers of the portion of capital actually there present. (Perry.)

Should a union succeed in shutting out competition and so unnaturally raising wages and lowering profits in some particular trade a twofold reaction tends to restore the natural equilibrium. An increased population will add to the supply of labour, while a diminished wage fund will lessen the demand for it. The joint action of these two principles will, sooner or later, overcome the power of any arbitrary organisation and restore profits and wages to their natural level. (Stirling.)

Against these barriers trade unions must dash themselves in vain. They are not to be broken through or eluded by any combinations, however unusual; for they are barriers set by Nature herself. (Cairnes.)

Trade unionism was confronted with the dilemma: whether it fails in its immediate aim, or it succeeds—the result would be unfavourable for the workers anyhow. If it fails in its demand for higher wages from the employer, then all organisational efforts, monetary expenditure and waste of energy will have been in vain; . . . while if it won, temporarily, an apparent success, then the final result would be still worse.

The violated natural laws will restore their authority through the medium of imminent reaction. The haughty mortal, who dares to counterpose his own personal will to divine influence, must inevitably be punished; his temporary prosperity vanishes, and he has to pay with long suffering for his transitory success. (James Stirling.)[1]

Briefly, the essence of all these professors' discoveries actually leads to the following: "Trade Unions and strikes can be of no use to the class of hired workmen." (Walker.) "Science knows no employers' profits." (Schultze von Delitsch.)

All these scientific arguments appear to us to-day simply comical; however, their propounders were the adepts of economic science of that period and their influence was so great that they even found their expression in the discussions organised by the General Council of the International Workingmen's Association. Marx formulated the political meaning of these scientific arguments very briefly in his speech against Weston:

> If, then, in enforcing a temporary rise of wages, the working men act foolishly, the capitalists, in enforcing a temporary fall of wages, would act not less foolishly.[2]

Marx realised the danger of these theoretics for the labour movement and therefore attacked the bourgeois economists and their socialist adherents with all the power of his mind and revolutionary passion. The first volume of *Capital* represents a crushing blow at the bourgeois authorities. Marx proved the falsity of the theory of the wages fund; he discovered the mystery of surplus value, he discovered the mystery of primitive accumulation, he proved by means of extensive and indisputable data how wages are determined, how value and surplus value are created, the difference between labour and labour power, etc. A theoretical dispute arose on the question of what the worker sells—his labour or his labour power—and the difference between labour and labour power. "Labour is the substance and the immanent measure of value, but has itself no value," [3] Marx writes. Basing himself on this definition Marx exposes the mystery of wages and the mystery of surplus value—"This is the corner-stone of the whole economic system of Karl Marx"

[1] See *Capital,* Vol. I, and Sydney and Beatrice Webb, *Industrial Democracy.*
[2] Marx, *Value, Price and Profit,* p. 11.
[3] *Capital,* Vol. 1, p. 588, Kerr, Chicago.

(Lenin). Marx writes: "If history took a long time to get at the bottom of the mystery of wages, nothing, on the other hand, is more easy to understand than the necessity, the *raison d'être,* of the *phenomenon.*" [1]

To this it is necessary to add that even after the discovery of this mystery, the struggle around this question never ceased for a moment, for the definition of Marx "that surplus value is the direct aim and the determining motive for capitalist production" touches on class interests, and as the old saying goes, "if geometrical axioms affected the interests of the people, these axioms would surely be denied" (Lenin). The extent to which the question of surplus value called forth disputes can be seen from the fact that of all the shabby professors, not one could be found who did not try to oppose Marx, and while doing so, some consciously, others unconsciously, made a mess of it. Sydney and Beatrice Webb belong to the scientists who unconsciously made a mess of it. They claim that Marx and Lassalle had demanded the right to the full product of labour. Such distortion of the viewpoint of Marx *roused the indignation* of the Russian translator, who made the following footnote: "The authors have a wrong conception of Marx, who determinedly opposed the doctrine of the right of the worker to the whole product of his labour. See *Critique of Gotha Programme.*" [2]

This modest note was written in 1898 by Lenin who translated this two-volume work of the Webbs in the village of Shushinsk, Minussinsky district (Siberia), together with N. Krupskaya.

Marx, in raising the banner of revolt against bourgeois economic science, knew that he dealt with serious problems: namely, will the working class follow theoretically and thus also politically in the footsteps of bourgeois political economy and politics, or will it forge its own theoretical weapon for the struggle against the ideology and policy of the capitalist class?

The problem of abstract theory became, as we see, a serious practical problem: is it necessary to set up trade unions, is it worth while to fight for shorter hours, what value has factory legislation for the working class?—in a word, *the question of the significance of partial demands for the general class struggle of the proletariat was thus raised.* Besides theory, the experiences

[1] *Ibid,* Vol. 1, p. 592.
[2] *Theory and Practice of British Trade Unionism,* Vol. 1, p. 325.

acquired in the struggles of the masses answered his question. This is why Marx in *Capital* constantly refers to the living experiences acquired in the struggle. Marx writes:

> The English factory workers were the champions, not only of the English, but of the modern working class generally, as their theorists were the first to throw down the gauntlet to the theory of Capital.[1]

The workers of the most advanced capitalist country of that period smashed, by means of their obdurate struggle, all statements of the bourgeois scientists. Marx, basing himself on experience and revolutionary theory, drove out all apologists of capital from the commanding heights of economic science.

Class trade union policy must have as its starting point the struggle for the shorter working day, for higher wages, the defence of female and child labour, extensive factory legislation, etc. However, in order to develop the struggle for these partial demands, one must understand their *rôle* and significance in the general class struggle of the proletariat. It is necessary to study the causes that gave rise to social legislation. In this respect Marx represents an astonishing phenomenon. He analysed a tremendous number of reports of English factory inspectors and all the anti-labour laws of England, Germany and France; he made a great issue of the problem of the eight-hour working day; he worked out principles to govern our attitude towards factory legislation, etc. It is sufficient to take the first volume of *Capital,* the major work of Marx, to see that the question of the purchase and sale of labour power, the value of labour power, the degree and forms of exploitation of labour power—are all given very much space. But Marx did not limit himself to devoting a great part of the first volume of *Capital* to the theoretical struggle against the bourgeois economists. Marx in this same volume of *Capital* gave a political reply to the question of what must be the attitude of the workers towards the struggle for their partial demands. In reply to the question of what the causes and sources of factory legislation are, Marx said:

> We see that only against its will, and under the pressure of the masses, did the English Parliament give up the laws against

[1] *Capital,* Vol. 1, p. 327, Kerr, Chicago.

Strikes and the Trade Unions, after it had itself, for five hundred years, held, with shameless egoism, the position of a permanent trades union of the capitalists against the labourers.[1]

Marx not only exposed the capitalist lust for exploiting the workers, for prohibiting association, prohibiting strikes, etc. From the very first days of his appearance on the political arena, he waged the struggle for the freedom of the unions, strikes, etc. This can be borne out by his literary-political activity, by all of his pamphlets, speeches and books even prior to the organisation of the International Workingmen's Association and prior to the publication of the first volume of *Capital*. The *Inaugural Address* of the International Workingmen's Association, drafted by Marx, begins with the following words:

Fellow Working Men. It is a great fact that the misery of the working masses has not diminished from 1848 to 1864.[2]

Then Marx writes the following about their conditions for getting labour legislation and its significance:

After a thirty years' struggle, fought with most admirable perseverance, the English working classes, improving a momentous split between the landlords and the money-lords, succeeded in carrying the Ten Hours Bill. The immense physical, moral and intellectual benefits hence accruing to the factory operatives, half yearly chronicled in the reports of the inspectors of factories, are now acknowledged on all sides. Most of the Continental Governments had to accept the English Factory Act in more or less modified forms, and the English Parliament itself is every year compelled to enlarge its sphere of action. . . . Hence the Ten Hours Bill was not only a great practical success, it was the victory of a principle; it was the first time that in broad daylight the political economy of the middle class succumbed to the political economy of the working class.[3]

We saw how highly Marx valued the obdurate struggle of the workers for shorter hours and for other achievements in this field. Not because he *overestimated* labour legislation, but

[1] *Ibid.*, p. 813.
[2] G. M. Stekloff: *History of the First International*, N.Y. and London, p. 439.
[3] *Ibid.*, *pp.* 443--44.

because he considered it necessary to fight determinedly against all *underestimation* of the struggle of the working masses for their immediate demands. Thus, the General Council of the International Workingmen's Association, on the proposal of Marx, drew up the following agenda for the Geneva Congress on July 21, 1865:

> (1) To consolidate, with the help of the Association, the efforts that are being made in the different countries for the struggle between Labour and Capital; (2) the trade unions, their past, present and future; (3) co-operative labour; (4) direct and indirect taxes; (5) shorter working hours; (6) female and child labour; (7) the Moscow invasion of Europe, and the restoration of an independent integral Poland; (8) the permanent armies, their influence on the interests of the working class.

From this we see that many of the points on the agenda are devoted to problems of the economic conditions of the working class. What is the reason for such an attitude towards the conditions of the working class? The reason is, as Engels wrote, that "the condition of the working class is the starting point of all social movements to-day."

At the following meeting of the General Council, Marx, on behalf of a special commission, recommended to the Congress in Geneva that an inquiry be made into the condition of the working class according to the following scheme:

> (1) Occupation; (2) age and sex of the employed; (3) number of employed; (4) hiring and wages; (4a) apprentices; (4b) wages, time or piece work, whether paid by middlemen—weekly, yearly, average earnings; (5) hours of work: hours of work in factories, hours of home work given out by small-scale employers, if the business is carried on in this way—night work, day work; (6) meal time and treatment; (7) conditions of places of work, overcrowding, ventilators, want of sunlight, use of gas light, etc., cleanliness; (8) nature of occupation; (9) effect of employment upon physical condition; (10) moral conditions, education; (11) character of trade, whether seasonal or more or less uniformly distributed over the year, whether output is destined principally for home or for foreign consumption.

This general table for inquiry was quite extensive and shows that Marx persistently worked on the question of the situation of the working class, and, contrary to the Proudhonists and Bakuninists, was interested in facts and not in declamations.

The programme of partial demands drafted by Marx for the Geneva Congress of the International Workingmen's Association is of special interest. This programme of demands, which ends with the section *Past, Present and Future of the Trade Unions* (see chapter *Rôle of the Trade Unions in the General Class Struggle of the Proletariat*), includes the following questions, besides those concerning the organisational structure of the International Workingmen's Association:

> The formation of mutual aid societies; statistical investigation into the conditions of the working class in all countries, to be carried out by the workers themselves; a detailed list of questions for collecting statistical data; a chapter devoted to the shortening of working hours and the establishment of the eight-hour working day; the prohibition of night work for women; child labour to be limited to two hours, four hours and six hours for children and adolescents, according to different ages; schooling of children to consist of mental, physical and technical training, "combining for children and adolescents paid productive labour with mental training, bodily exercise and technical instruction."

This same report devotes a special chapter to the creation of co-operatives. The report emphasises that the aim of the International Workingmen's Association is to counteract the "intrigues of the capitalists, who are always prepared, in case of a strike or lock-out, to utilize foreign-born workers as a weapon with which to stifle the just demands of the native workers," to "combine, unify and co-ordinate the still scattered efforts which are made in the different countries for the liberation of the working class, not only to develop among the workers of the different countries a sense of fraternity, but to get them to convert this sense into action, also to close their ranks for the purpose of forming an army of liberation." If we take into account the fact that the report also contained a special section on direct and indirect taxes, a section on "the necessity of destroying Russian influence in Europe, on establishing the right of nations to self-determination and the restoration of Poland on a democratic and social basis," a section on the "harmful influence of the standing armies," and that this report contains the famous slogan: "He who

H

does no work, neither shall he eat," we get an idea of the nature of this document, which actually served as the starting point for programmes of concrete demands to be drafted in all capitalist countries.

Why did Marx consider it necessary to draw up such a detailed programme for the Geneva Congress? Why did he raise the economic demands of the proletariat as the central question? Marx himself explains this in his letter to Kugelmann, dated October 9, 1866, in the following way:

> I deliberately restricted it (the programme) to those points which allow of immediate agreement and concerted action by the *workers* and give direct nourishment and impetus to the requirements of the class struggle and the *organisation of the workers into a class.*[1]

Marx again appears before us as statesman and tactician. His aim is to get the workers to agree to *joint action,* correctly seeing in this the prerequisite for "organising the workers into a class." Here we are particularly struck by Marx's great genius as a tactician who knows exactly what link to grasp during any given moment, under concrete circumstances, in order to rally the masses and lead them to battle. Our Communist Parties and revolutionary trade unions should learn more of this remarkable tactical art of Karl Marx.

The Geneva Congress of the International Workingmen's Association resolved:

> Limitation of the working day is a preliminary condition in the absence of which all further attempts at improvement and emancipation must prove abortive. We propose eight hours as the legal limit of the working day.

The slogan of the eight-hour working day, which afterwards came to be the slogan of the whole international proletariat, was raised at a time when in all capitalist countries, with the exception of England, the working day lasted as long as fourteen hours. We see that the First International raised slogans based on the general tendencies of development of the labour movement and

---

[1] Marx, *Letters to Kugelmann,* p. 39.

not only on day-to-day questions of that period. We cannot but mention here that at the congresses of the Comintern and the R.I.L.U. there were Communists who came out against the seven-hour day on the ground that the working day in some countries and some industries lasts in reality nine to ten hours.

Marx attached exceptionally great significance to laws providing for the shortening of the working day and factory legislation, fighting against the Bakuninists, who wrote about the futility of factory legislation in the bulletin of the Jura Federation:

> "The creation of a normal working day," Marx writes, "is, therefore, the product of a protracted civil war, more or less dissembled between the capitalist class and the working class ... [1] For 'protection' against the 'serpent of their agonies' the labourers must put their heads together, and, as a class, compel the passing of a law, an all-powerful *social barrier* that shall prevent the very workers from selling, by voluntary contract with capital, themselves and their families into slavery and death." [2]

How remote this viewpoint of Marx on the labour laws is from the haughty (Marx would have said "transcendental") declamations of the Bakuninists on the uselessness of labour laws!

The struggle of the Communists for partial demands, as well as their programme after seizing power, served as a pretext for the anarchists to accuse Marx and the Marxists of "bourgeois narrowness" and of giving up the revolution; they intentionally confused the critics of Marx with Marx, passing revisionism for Marxism. The anarchists placed the question of the State in the centre and from this angle vilified and slandered Marx and Marxism. It is very characteristic in this regard to note the "criticism" by the anarchist Cherkezov of the ten points in the *Communist Manifesto* which (according to Marx and Engels) the proletariat will have to carry out after the workers' revolution as soon as it becomes the ruling class.

[1] Marx, *Capital,* Vol. 1, Kerr, Chicago, p. 327.
[2] *Ibid.,* p. 330.

MARX AND ENGELS	CHERKEZOV
(1) Expropriation of landed property and application of all land rent to public purposes.	(1) All land to the State! In Turkey the land is the property of the State of the Sultan, who hands over part of it to his loyal subjects.
(4) Confiscation of the property of all emigrants and rebels.	(4) Old infamy, practised by all despots and oppressors.
(8) Compulsory labour for all.	(8) A shocking demand, borrowed from the Paraguayan Jesuits.[1]

I do not give here the other "profoundly critical" remarks of Cherkezov, who tries to prove that the *Communist Manifesto* is nothing more than literary plagiarism. This accusation is enough to prove the degree of "revolutionariness" of the stars of Russian anarchism, who consider the confiscation of the property of emigrants and rebels "an infamy." To make the picture more complete, it is necessary to note also that this same Cherkezov raves against partial demands, arguing that demands like the eight-hour working day, the prohibition of paying wages in kind, the responsibility of the employer to compensate for the complete or partial disability of the workers, etc., are all "pieces of labour legislation of the bourgeois state, and have nothing in common with real socialism."

This difference in attitude towards the struggle for the workers' immediate demands was reflected both in the scientific and practical work of Marx and his Proudhonist and Bakuninist opponents. Marx collected his material with maximum persistence and built his conclusions on the firm basis of facts. Marx first of all analysed the situation and the facts, and only then drew his conclusions—a feature absolutely unknown to the Anarcho-Syndicalist theoreticians.

The great significance that Marx attached to the need for ascertaining the conditions of the working class can be seen from the detailed questionnaire for workers drawn up by him

[1] See Cherkezov, *Forerunners of the International* (Russian edition), "A Doctrine of Marxism" pp. 56-87, Moscow, 1912.

in 1880 and published in his preface in *La Revue Socialiste* of April 20, 1881. Marx says the following about this questionnaire:

Not a single government (monarchist or bourgeois-republican) has ever dared to make a serious investigation concerning the conditions of the French working class. Yet how many investigations relating to crises in agriculture, finances, industry, commerce and politics have been instituted.

The infamies of capitalist exploitation, exposed in the official investigations instituted by the British government; the legislation which these revelations compelled to be passed (limitation by law of the working day to ten hours, and the law concerning female and child labour, etc.), have made the French bourgeoisie still more fearful of the dangers which such an impartial and systematic investigation might conjure up.

In the hope that, perhaps, we might be able to induce the Republican government to follow the example of the monarchist government of England and also organise an extensive investigation into the deeds and misdeeds of capitalist exploitation, we shall endeavour to launch such a questionnaire with the meagre funds at our disposal. In this we hope to receive the support of all urban and rural workers, who realise that they alone, with full knowledge of the causes, can describe the misery which they endure, that they alone, and no redeemer sent by Providence, can energetically apply the remedies to the social maladies from which they suffer. We count also on the socialists of all schools, who, desiring social reforms, must know *exactly* and *positively* the conditions under which the working class, to which the future belongs, works and comes into motion.

This collection of labour data (*Cahiers du travail*) is the first task which socialist democracy must perform in order to prepare the social renovation.[1]

The questionnaire itself represents a carefully elaborated document, from all points of view, deserving the most serious study. Marx took the questions which had been raised by him in 1865 and 1866 as the basis of this questionnaire, but in view of the fact that he aimed at explaining to the workers and to the French socialists themselves the organic connections that

[1] *La Revue Socialiste*, April 20, 1880, No. 4, pp. 193-94. Reprinted in *Communist Internatioal* No. 3/4, 1933, and in pamphlet form.

existed between politics and economics—and this was and is the weakest spot in the revolutionary labour movement of France—he considerably extended the questionnaire, including also a number of leading questions. One hundred questions in the questionnaire cover the forms of wages, the length of the working day, labour protection, the cost of living, forms of settling conflicts, forms of mutual aid, forms of interference by the State authorities in the struggle between Labour and Capital, forms of voluntary and compulsory mutual aid societies, number and nature of resistance societies, character and duration of strikes, etc. Such a questionnaire which raised the question of labour protection laws and the intimate connection between economics and politics, etc., was of tremendous importance for the Proudhon-Blanquist traditions of the French labour movement. Serious investigation of conditions in at least a few scores of factories along the lines of this questionnaire could have given very valuable material for concretising the tactics of the revolutionary movement of that period; however, the questionnaire was published in a magazine with a circulation of 25,000 copies, and was afterwards forgotten.

Marx always paid close attention to what was going on in the midst of the working masses, and on the basis of this would verify his tactics. Friedrich Lessner, in his reminiscences, writes:

> Marx always tried to come in contact with workers and to converse with them. The opinions of rank-and-file workers were of great interest to him!

Marx listened to what the workers had to say, tried to grasp their thoughts and see how they reacted to their surroundings. He realised that not all of his works could be understood by the average worker, but he knew that his teachings were the conscious expression of an unconscious historical process. Marx, when coming in contact with the workers, tested himself, and the force of his genius formulated just what the worker instinctively felt. Fighting for the workers' partial demands, Marx knew the *rôle* that they played in the general class struggle of the proletariat. About this we read in the *Communist Manifesto:*

The Communists fight for the attainment of the immediate aims, for the enforcement of the momentary interests of the working class, but in the movement of the present they also represent and take care of the future of that movement.[1]

This is what explains the fact that Marx always kept level with the movement of his time and always put forward the actual slogans of the day.

[1] *Communist Manifesto*, p. 34. Martin Lawrence, Ltd.

CHAPTER VIII

Marx and the Strike Movement

FIGHTING against the overestimation as well as underestimation of the economic struggle and the trade unions, Marx and Engels paid maximum attention to strikes and the economic struggle of the proletariat. Both Marx and Engels considered the strike a powerful weapon of struggle for the immediate and ultimate aims of the working class. The transformation of the scattered workers into a class which proceeded during the course of a desperate struggle is classically described in the *Communist Manifesto*—this vivid and unfading document of world communism. The *Communist Manifesto* graphically describes the birth of the bourgeoisie and its grave-digger—"the modern working class—a class of labourers who live only so long as they find work, and who find work only so long as their labour increases capital."[1]

Here is what we read in the *Communist Manifesto* on the ways and means of "organising the proletariat into a class":

> The proletariat goes through various stages of development. With its birth begins its struggle with the bourgeoisie. At first the contest is carried on by individual labourers, then by the work people of a factory, then by the operatives of one trade, in one locality, against the individual bourgeois, who directly exploits them. They direct their attacks not against the bourgeois conditions of production, but against the instruments of production themselves; they destroy imported wares that compete with their labour, they smash to pieces machinery, they set factories ablaze, they seek to restore by force the vanished status of the workman of the Middle Ages.
>
> At this stage the labourers still form an incoherent mass, scattered over the whole country, and broken up by their mutual competition. . . .

[1] *Communist Manifesto*, p. 22.

But with the development of industry the proletariat not only increases in number; it becomes concentrated in greater masses, its strength grows, and it feels that strength more! . . . the collisions between individual workmen and individual bourgeois take more and more the character of collisions between two classes. Thereupon the workers begin to form combinations (trades unions) against the bourgeois; they club together in order to keep up the rate of wages; they found permanent associations in order to make provision beforehand for these occasional revolts. Here and there the contest breaks out into riots.

Now and then the workers are victorious, but only for a time. The real fruit of their battle lies, not in the immediate result, but in the ever-expanding union of the workers. This union is helped on by the improved means of communication that are created by modern industry, and that places the workers of different localities in contact with one another. It was just this contact that was needed to centralise the numerous local struggles, all of the same character, into one national struggle between classes. But every class struggle is a political struggle.

This organisation of the proletarians into a class, and consequently into a political party, is continually being upset again by the competition between the workers themselves. But it ever rises up again, stronger, firmer, mightier.[1]

In his book, *Condition of the Working Class in England in 1844*, Engels devotes much space to the unceasing struggle of the British working class to improve its condition. He considers strikes a school of war, a necessary and compulsory weapon in the struggle for the emancipation of the working class. Engels studied the conditions and the struggle of the British proletariat in the first decades of the nineteenth century, when the workers' struggles were to a considerable degree spontaneous in character. Strong revolutionary sensitiveness was required for anyone to find his way in the maze of events of that time and correctly to appraise the true character of the strike movement that went on while the workers were being vilified to the utmost by "impartial" bourgeois scientists. Here is what Engels writes:

In war the injury of one party is the benefit of the others, and

[1] *Communist Manifesto,* pp. 14-18.

since workingmen are on a war footing towards their employers, they do merely what great potentates do when they seize each other by the throat. . . .

The incredible frequency of these strikes proves best of all to what extent the social war has broken out all over England. . . . These strikes, at first skirmishes, sometimes result in weighty struggles; they decide nothing, it is true, but they are the strongest proof that the decisive battle between bourgeoisie and proletariat is approaching. They are the school of war of the workingmen in which they prepare themselves for the great struggle which cannot be avoided; they are the pronunciamentos of single branches of industry that these too have joined the labour movement. . . . And as schools of war they are unexcelled. In them is developed the peculiar courage of the English. . . .

It is in truth no trifle for a workingman, who knows want from experience, to face it with his wife and children, to ensure hunger and wretchedness for months together, and to stand firm and unshaken through it all. What is death, what the galleys which await the French revolutionist, in comparison with gradual starvation, with the daily sight of a starving family, with the certainty of future revenge on the part of the bourgeoisie, all of which the English workingman chooses in preference to subjection under the yoke of the property-holding class. . . . People who endure so much to bend one single bourgeois will be able to break the power of the whole bourgeoisie.[1]

Engels, as we see, emphasises that the strike is one of the varieties of social war, that strikes are indispensable as a school of war. He fights against the underestimation of strikes, against verbal revolutionism, against a haughty, disdainful attitude towards the economic struggle of the workers, he stresses that great stores of courage, self-sacrifice, devotion and firmness are necessary for strikes and that the army of the proletariat is created and forged precisely in these preliminary battles. This viewpoint of Engels was shared by Marx.

The great importance that Marx attached to the strike movement and the organisation of solidarity among the strikers, to the struggle against bringing the blacklegs from other countries, can be seen from the minutes of the General Council of the International Workingmen's Association. These minutes, despite their

[1] Engels, *Condition of the Working Class in England in 1844.*

brevity, clearly show how much attention Marx and the First International founded by him paid to the task of rallying the trade unions and getting them to render help to the strikers. Here are a few excerpts from these minutes:

On April 25, 1865, a letter was read from the compositors of Leipzig referring to their strike and expressing the hope that the London compositors would assist them. The General Council sends a delegation composed of Fox, Marx and Cremer to attend a meeting of the Compositors' Society of London and to inform them of the letter from Leipzig. On May 9, 1865, Fox gave a report of the fact that the delegation had been to the meeting of the compositors, but that the London compositors declared that it was not possible to grant money for a period of three months, so that the delegation had therefore failed in its effort. On May 23, 1865, a letter was read from Lyons from the workers of the tulle factories, in connection with an attack upon their wages. On June 20, 1865, a report was heard to the effect that the Lille weavers' society would most likely join the I.W.A. Then also a letter from Lyons was read where it was stated that the workers had to retreat as a result of the shortage of means for existence. On January 30, 1866, attention was called to the fact that the London trade union was discussing the question of Boards of Arbitration. On March 27 a report was made on the strike of the tailors in London and that in London they now intended to get men from the Continent to supplant those on strike. The General Council decided that the Continental Secretaries be informed, with the view to keep continental workmen away from London during the struggle. On April 4, 1866, a delegate from the wire-makers thanked the Council for its attempts to prevent the employers from getting workers from the Continent to take the place of the strikers. On May 22 a letter from Geneva was read on the outbreak of a strike among the bootmakers, and the request to inform all workers. The Geneva Strikers' Committee requested that communications to this effect should be sent to other countries. A delegation was then elected to set up contacts with the Stratford Lodge of bricklayers and cabinetmakers, who "promised to join the Association" not in words but in deeds. On September 28, 1869, a letter was read from the paper-stainers of New York, asking the Council to use its influence to prevent the importation of men to defeat the workers now on strike. Then also a letter was read from the silk-printers and block-cutters of Hilden, asking help because of a strike, and also a letter from the basket-makers, in connection with a lockout. The Secretary was instructed to reply that there was no prospect of financial help. On October 12, 1869, a letter was read concerning the strike of the wool spinners in Elboeuf, the latter asking for help. The spinners insisted upon a list of fixed prices. On November 26, 1869, Marx communicated that he had received a letter from Hanover, where the engineers had been out on strike for six weeks against the lengthening of the working day and reduction in wages. On January 4, 1870, in reply to the request of the Executive of the Social-Democratic Party for loans for the miners of Waldenburg now on strike, the secretaries were instructed to reply that "there were no prospects of help from London." On January 11, 1870, a letter was read from Nouveille-sur-Saône, asking for help for the cotton-printers on strike. The secretary was instructed to communicate with Manchester concerning this strike. On April 18, 1870, a letter from Varlin states that he had been to Lille to inaugurate a trade union organisation under the auspices of the Association. Then also Dupont called attention to the severe sentences passed upon the miners as a result of the strike. Dupont and Marx were appointed to draw up a special appeal. The meeting of the General Council on May 31, 1870, received a delegation from the striking ironfounders of Paris. On June 14, 1870, the secretary reported that the Amalgamated Engineers had proposed a levy of twopence throughout the Association for the ironfounders on strike in Paris. On June 21, 1870, the General Council discussed the Geneva lock-out. In connection with the lock-out Marx was appointed to draft an appeal to all working-class organisations and branches of the Association on the continent of Europe and the United States, calling for aid to strikers. On June 20, 1870, a communication was read to the effect that the Amalgamated Engineers had resolved to make a loan to the ironfounders of Paris. The Council resolved that the secretary of the Engineers bring the money to Paris not only to ensure its safe delivery, but because of the "good moral effects." [1]

These few excerpts from the minutes of the General Council bear witness to the important *rôle* that questions of strikes and the struggle against strike-breaking, etc., play in the work of the First International. This does not mean that the General Council occupied itself only with such questions. The General

[1] Archives of Marx-Engels-Lenin Institute. Minutes of the General Council.

Council of the First International occupied itself also with great political problems. But one of the specific traits of the First International consisted in the fact—and this is doubtless one of the great merits of Marx—that at meetings of the General Council problems of the strike struggles received much attention, and that there was no artificial dividing line between politics and economics—both were discussed, decisions were adopted on both questions and often "Dr. Marx" was very modestly instructed to go to some meeting of a trade union, to draw up a leaflet in connection with some strike, to write to some specific country and call upon its workers to wage a campaign against the sending of strike-breakers, etc. Marx very correctly considered this to be an integral part of his general political activity.

The significance that Marx attached to these questions can be seen from the following instance. On April 23, 1866, Marx wrote to Engels:

> The situation in the International is as follows: Since my return discipline has been completely restored. Besides, the successful interference by the International in the tailors strike (by means of letters of the secretaries for France, Belgium, etc.) caused a sensation among the local trade unions.[1]

This interference of the International in strikes made it extremely popular. The workers from all countries began to write to the International whenever they discovered difficulties. On March 22, 1867, Marx was happy to write to Engels:

> Our International celebrated a great victory. We secured monetary aid for the striking bronze workers of Paris from the British trade unions. As soon as the bosses saw this they gave in. This business has caused a great deal of noise in the French papers, and we are now an established force in France.[2]

In some sections of the employers, legendary rumours began to spread about the force and power of the International Workingmen's Association. Marx attached great importance to giving practical aid in the struggle of the workers against capitalism.

[1] Marx and Engels, *Complete Works* (German edition), Part III, Vol. 3, p. 327.
[2] *Ibid.*, p. 378.

At the Geneva Congress of the International, in 1866, he submitted the following resolution:

> One of the special functions of the Association, which has already been executed on different occasions with great success, is to oppose the intrigues of the capitalists, who are always ready in case of stoppage or lock-out to misuse workers of foreign lands as instruments for frustrating the demands of the native workers. . . . This is one of the major aims of the Association . . . that the workers of the different countries should not only feel like brothers but also know how to act as united parts of the army of emancipation. (*Resolution on International Mutual Aid in the Struggle of Labour Against Capital.*) [1]

The significance attached by Marx to the question of strikes and practical solidarity in connection with strikes can be gathered, for example, from his letter to Engels of August 18, 1869. In this letter he expressed his pleasure because the Paris bronze workers had returned the forty-five pounds that they had borrowed. Further on he writes:

> In Posen, as Zabicky informs us, the Polish workers (carpenters, etc.) have emerged victorious from their strike through the aid rendered them by their Berlin fellow workers. This struggle against *Monsieur le Capital*—even in the subordinate form of a strike—disposes of national prejudices in a manner quite different from the bourgeoisie ranting about peace.[2]

We have read a number of appeals, written by Marx upon the instructions of the General Council, in connection with large-scale strikes of that period. Thus, for example, Marx drafted the appeal to the workers of Europe and the United States concerning the mass murders in 1869; the striking puddlers and miners in St. Etienne and Fremeriés (Belgium): Marx pillories the "heroic impetuousness" of the Belgian cavalry at St. Etienne and the "unshakable driving power" of the Belgian infantry in Fremeriés; he writes that "some politicians trace these incredible deeds to motives of sublime patriotism," that the Belgian capitalist is famous for his eccentric passion for

---

[1] Stegmann, *Handbuch des Sozialismus*, p. 344.
[2] Marx and Engels, *Complete Works* (German ed.), Part III, Vol. 4, p. 224.

what he calls "liberty of labour." Marx ridiculed the fact that the members of the International in Belgium had been arrested on the charge of "belonging to an Association founded for the purpose of attacking the lives and property of individuals. . . ." He characterises the Belgian Constitutionalists as follows:

> There is but one small country in the civilised world where the war power exists solely to butcher striking workers, where every strike is eagerly and with malicious joy turned into an official pretext for massacring the workers. That country of single blessedness is Belgium, the model state of continental constitutionalism, the smug, well-hedged paradise of the landlord, the capitalist and the priest.
>
> The earth is not more certain to perform its annual revolution than the Belgian government its yearly massacre of workers. This year's massacre does not differ from that of last year except in the ghastly number of its holocaust, the more hideous atrocities of an otherwise ridiculous military, the noisier jubilation of the clerical and capitalist press and the more insolent frivolousness of the pretext advanced by the government's butchers.[1]

This brilliant leaflet ends with a call to collect funds to help the families of the strikers and to defray "the expenses incident upon the legal defence of the arrested workmen and the inquiry proposed by the Brussels Committee."

This is not the only leaflet written by Marx. Marx wrote a leaflet in connection with the lockout of the building workers in Geneva in 1870, calling on the building trades workers of all countries to "render moral and material aid in their struggle against capitalist despotism." The appeal exhorts all workers not to permit blacklegging and to realise the fact that the "labour problem is not a temporary and local problem, but a problem of world historic significance."

On the instructions of the General Council Marx drafted a leaflet on behalf of the striking German tailors in London, addressed to their colleagues in Germany. In this leaflet Marx, among other things, defines "collective agreement," a definition that characterises Marx's attitude towards questions of the

---

[1] Leaflet issued by the General Council of the International Workingmen's Association entitled *Belgian Massacre*. See *Vorbote*, 1869, pp. 87-91.

economic struggle. "The agreement proposed by the employers has been accepted by the workers," Marx writes, "but this agreement of April 6 can be considered only a truce." [1]

Of exceptional interest, from the point of view of Marx's appraisal of the strike movement, is the report written by him for the Fourth Congress of the International Workingmen's Association held in Basle in 1869:

> The report of your General Council [writes Marx] will mainly relate to the guerilla fights *between Capital and Labour*—we mean the *strikes which, during the last year, have perturbed the continent of Europe* and were said to have sprung neither from the misery of the labourer nor from the despotism of the capitalist, but from secret intrigues of our Association. [2]

Further on Marx speaks about the "economic revolt" of the Basle workers and about the fact that the "Norman weavers rose against the encroachment of Capital," in spite of the fact that they had not had any organisation. Thanks to the intervention of the International Association the London workers responded to this strike. "It gave rise to the birth of trade unions at Rouen, Elboeuf and Doriatal and their environs and it sealed anew the bond of fraternity between the English and French workingclass."

Further on Marx continues:

> The dance of economic revolts was opened at Lyons by the silk winders, most of them females. In their distress they appealed to the International which, mainly by the aid of its members, helped them to carry the day. . . . At Lyons, as before at Rouen, the female workers played a noble and prominent part in the movement. . . . Other Lyons trades have since followed in the track of the silk winders. Since ten thousand new members were thus gained by us in a few weeks from among that heroic population, which more than thirty years ago inscribed upon its banner the watchword of the modern proletariat: *"Vivre en travaillant, ou mourir en combattant"* (Either live and work or die fighting). [3]

---

[1] Archives, Marx-Engels-Lenin Institute, Moscow.

[2] Marx, Report of General Council of the I.W.A. to its Fourth General Congress in Basle. Reprinted in *Communist International No.* 5/6, 1933, p. 156. *Vorbote,* 1869, p. 133.

[3] *Vorbote,* 1869, p. 140, Marx's Report to the Basle Congress.

Marx further describes the struggle and persecution of the workers in Austria, Prussia and Hungary and gives an interesting example of how the Hungarian Minister for Home Affairs, von Wenckheim, "puffing and blowing at his cigar," questioned the workers' delegation which came to him to get permission to open a club:

> Are you a workman? Do you work hard? For nothing else you have to care. You do not want public clubs and if you dabble in politics, we shall know what measure to take against you. I shall do nothing for you. Let the workmen grumble to their hearts' content.[1]

Passing over to England Marx wrote:

> No wonder, then, that England also had this year to boast of its own workmen's massacre [among the Welsh coal miners.— A.L.]. The Welsh jury were a narrowly prejudiced class jury, and brought in a verdict of justifiable homicide.[2]

This report to the Basle Congress is of great interest, for here Marx gathered many facts not only concerning the strike movement of the period, but also concerning the repressions against the members of the International Workingmen's Association.

The interference of the First International in the strike movement caused alarm among the bourgeoisie of all countries: the Geneva employers growled that the local members of the International were ruining the Canton of Geneva by submitting to decrees sent from London. In Basle the capitalists "transformed at once their private feuds with their men into a State crusade against the International Workingmen's Association." They dispatched a special messenger with the fantastic commission of ascertaining the dimensions of the general "treasury box" of the International. We read in the report to the Basle Congress that an official Brussels investigator thought it hidden in a certain strongbox kept in a secret place. He got at it, opened it forcibly and lo! it contained only some pieces of coal. Marx ironically adds: "Perhaps touched by the hand of the police the pure gold of the International turns at once into coal."

[1] *Ibid.*, p. 161.   [2] *Ibid.*, p. 142.

I

The government Press of France, "paid as it is to mis-state and misinterpret unpleasant facts," reported that the strikes were called on the secret orders of the central Council and its emissaries, and hinted broadly that the International was in the service of a foreign government, while the strike was the result of some foreign Machiavelli, who had known how to win the good graces of this all-powerful Association.[1]

After the Commune and the famous appeal of the International Workingmen's Association, the slanders multiplied. In the report to the Hague Congress, in 1872, Marx quoted dozens of facts, illustrating the fury and malice against the International Workingmen's Association. Jules Favre, immediately after the suppression of the Commune, sent a note to all the governments recommending joint action against the International. Bismarck and the Pope of Rome immediately responded and a meeting took place between the Emperors of Austria and Germany in Salzburg to draw up measures against the International Workingmen's Association.

Marx, in his report to the Hague Congress, wrote:

> However, all measures of repression which the ingenuity of various European governments could devise, pale before the campaign of slander which was launched by the lying power of the civilised world. Apocryphal stories and secrets of the International, shameless forgery of public documents and private letters, sensational telegrams, etc., follow one upon another: all the floodgates of calumny which the mercenary bourgeois press had at its disposal were suddenly thrown open and let loose a cataclysm of defamation designed to engulf the hated foe. This campaign of calumny does not possess its match in history, so truly international is the scene on which it is enacted, and so complete is the agreement with which the most various party organs of the ruling classes conduct it. After the great fire in Chicago, the news was sent round the world by telegram that this fire was the hellish act of the International, and indeed it is to be wondered at that the hurricane which devastated the West Indies was not likewise attributed to this same satanic influence.[2]

---

[1] *C.I.*, 5/6, 1933, p. 159.
[2] Archives, Marx-Engels-Lenin Institute. Reprinted in *C.I.* 5-6, 1933, p. 165.

"Instructions" from London, secret emissaries, heaps of gold, forgery of documents and streams of slander and vilification—how modern it all is and how this same struggle, only on a broader scale, is being carried on by the international bourgeoisie against the Comintern to-day! To the ravings of international capital, their correspondents from the secret service departments and their spies, Marx replied: "It is not the International that threw the workers into strikes, but on the contrary, the strikes threw the workmen into the arms of the International." [1]

The Proudhonists and Bakuninists, as is known, had originally been against the trade unions and against strikes, but afterwards they turned through 180 degrees and became energetic defenders of the trade unions, considering them the only form for workers' associations, and strikes as the only form of struggle. On the question of strikes, Bakunin based himself on the premise that "economic demands form the sum and substance of the International" and that "resistance funds and trade unions form the only effective means of struggle, which at the present time the workers can have at their disposal against the bourgeoisie." Adhering to this absolute basis—Bakunin always thought in the absolute and did not understand dialectics—he announced his formulation of the significance and development of the strike movement. Here is what Bakunin wrote:

> The strike is the beginning of the social war between the proletariat and the bourgeoisie, so far still within the framework of the law. Strikes represent a valuable method of struggle from two angles: first of all, they electrify the masses, steel their moral energy and rouse in their hearts the consciousness of the deep antagonism between their interests and the interests of the bourgeoisie: every day they come to see more and more vividly the precipice that separates them from this class: and, secondly, they greatly facilitate the awakening of the consciousness and the establishment of solidarity between the workers of all trades, of all localities and all countries—such is the dual effect, on the one hand negative and on the other hand positive, which aims directly at creating a new proletarian world, placing it almost completely in opposition to the bourgeois world.

[1] *Vorbote,* 1869, p. 138. Reprinted in *C.I.* 5-6, 1933.

Who does not know how much the workmen are obliged to suffer and sacrifice in each and every strike? However, strikes are necessary; so necessary that without them it would be impossible either to rouse the masses of the people for the social struggle or to organise them. The strike is a war, and the masses organise only during times of war and by means of war, which wrests every workman away from his usual, senseless, desolate and hopeless solitude; war suddenly united him with all other workmen in the name of the same desire, the same purpose, and convinces all in a most graphic and tangible way of the necessity to organise on a solid basis if they want to emerge victorious. The indignant masses are as molten metal which is poured and fused into one solid mass and can be formed more easily than cold metal, *provided good masters are found who can fuse it according to the properties and laws* inherent in the given metal, in accordance with the demands and instincts of the masses.

Strikes awaken all social-revolutionary instincts in the masses, which are concealed in the inner recesses of every workman; as a matter of fact they form his historical social-psychological being; however, in usual times, under the yoke of slave habits and general humility, he confesses to only very few of them. But when these instincts, roused by the economic struggle, awaken in the midst of the working masses, the propagation of social-revolutionary ideas among them becomes extremely easy. For these ideas are nothing but the purest and truest expression of the instincts of the people. . . .

Every strike is all the more valuable since it extends and deepens the gulf between the bourgeois class and the masses, for it proves to the workmen in the plainest way the absolute incompatibility of their interests with the interests of the capitalists and owners. . . . As a matter of fact, there is no better means of wresting the workmen away from the political influence of the bourgeoisie than a strike. . . .

Yes, the strike is a great weapon; it creates, multiplies, organises and forms the workers' troops—troops that will have to conquer and smash the bourgeois state power and prepare a broad and free soil for a new world.[1]

If we compare these lyrics, which include also some correct points, with what Marx writes in his first volume of *Capital*, we shall at once see the difference between the dialectician and the

[1] Quotation from G. M. Stekloff, *Bakunin* (Russian ed.), Vol. III, pp. 287-91.

metaphysician. Marx writes about *concrete* strikes, gives dozens of examples of workers' actions, describes what influence these had on working hours, wages, labour legislation, etc. Bakunin is not interested in factory laws, for he does not see the connection between partial demands and the final goal. He thinks that every strike may develop into a revolution. Marx is interested in the scope within which the trade union can act, Bakunin does not bother about this. Bakunin treated the question of strikes the same as all the anarchists treated the question of the State, about which Lenin writes in his *State and Revolution*. The points that are correct in the anarchist programme concerning the question of the State—the final aim, a society with neither classes nor State—the anarchists mixed with so much metaphysical syrup that they drowned the very possibility of ever reaching this stage in the development of humanity. The same with regard to the strike—they ascribed so many miraculous virtues to it—the anarchists fairly rave about the strike as "the redeemer"—that it is hard to define its character and scope, its limits, its consequences and its relation to other forms of struggle. What then is the scope of action of the trade unions and of strikes? Marx replied to this exhaustively in his dispute with Weston:

> At the same time and quite apart from the general servitude involved in the wages system, the working class ought not to exaggerate to themselves the ultimate working of these everyday struggles. They ought not to forget that they are fighting with effects, but not with the causes of those effects; that they are retarding the downward movement, but not changing its direction; that they are applying palliatives, not curing the malady. They ought, therefore, not to be exclusively absorbed in these unavoidable guerilla fights incessantly springing up from the never-ceasing encroachments of Capital or changes of the market. They ought to understand that, with all the miseries it imposes upon them, the present system simultaneously engenders the *material conditions and the social forms* necessary for an economic reconstruction of society. Instead of the *conservative* motto, "A fair day's wages for a fair day's work!" they ought to inscribe on their banner the revolutionary watchword, "Abolition of the wages system!" [1]

Here we have come to one of the central points in the teachings

[1] Marx, *Value, Price and Profit*, pp. 92-8.

of Marx on strikes. We have already seen that Marx and Engels referred to strikes as "social war," as "economic revolt," "real civil war," "guerilla war," "school of war," "advance guard collisions," that they wrote about strikes being dangerous for the régime, etc., and now Marx writes that the economic strike is a "struggle against effects and not against causes, that it is a palliative, but not a cure." Is there not some contradiction here, or perhaps Marx changed his original viewpoint? No, neither the one nor the other. The fact is that on the question of strikes, Marx had to deal blows to the *"Right"* and *"Left."* Among the British trade unions at that time the opinion crystallised that strikes were disadvantageous to the workers. "We believe," said Allan, one of the leaders of the trade unions, to the Royal Commission in 1867, "that strikes are a senseless, ridiculous waste of money not only for the workers, but also for the employer." [1]

Marx energetically fought against the bourgeois theory that strikes were simply a waste of forces and means, proving the vast significance of strikes for turning the proletariat into a class. On the other hand, anarcho-syndicalist ideas began to spread in the ranks of the First International to the effect that the economic strike was the *only* means of struggle. This is why Marx sharply raised that question, saying that the task was to direct the energy of the masses to struggle against the *causes* of exploitation, though recognising at the same time the importance of the struggle against the *effects* of exploitation.

In the letter to Bolte which we quoted above, Marx indicated how individual economic demands of the workers develop into political movements, *i.e.,* into the movement of a class. Here more than ever before quantity rapidly changes into quality. From all the teachings of Marx and Engels we see that economic collisions are of great political significance; however, the point is the degree, the proportion of this significance. If an economic strike bears the nature of a spontaneous outburst, it does not lose its political significance because of this—"spontaneity is the primitive form of consciousness" (Lenin). The political significance of this strike depends upon the size and scope of the movement. Even where the strike is on a broad scale, if the leaders from the very outset lead it into narrow craft channels

---

[1] Gustav Jaeckh, *Die Internationale,* Leipzig, 1904.

the political edge of the strike is blunted and it is immediately deprived of its chief content—it can no longer yield the political results which it could have yielded originally; if a strike which has purely economic demands as its point of departure is from the very beginning consciously directed along the line of combining it with the political struggle, it yields maximum effects. Marx knew that the economic strike was an important weapon in the hands of the proletariat against the bourgeoisie, since everything that deals a blow to the capitalists deals a blow also to the capitalist system. He considered it necessary and important to emphasise that a narrow and limited economic struggle "cannot change the direction of capitalist development."

From this conception of Marx, that a purely economic struggle is a struggle against effect, but not against causes, some attempted to create the theory that before the war all economic strikes had been of a defensive character and only since the beginning of the general crisis of capitalism have all strikes acquired an offensive character. This idea can be found in the book of Fritz David, *Bankruptcy of Reformism,* rich in facts and statistics, but containing a number of incorrect formulations. Such a classification of economic strikes into defensive and offensive strikes is incorrect and politically harmful, for it is not based on real life; for real life tells us that prior to the war there had been offensive strikes (strikes for higher wages, shorter working hours), while to-day also defensive strikes are waged. It is wrong to divide defensive and offensive movements according to periods of time; they must be classified according to the analysis of every concrete strike, the action of the trade union and the *rôle* of the workers in that strike. It is possible to fight against the effects of capitalism by defensive as well as offensive means.

The viewpoint of Marx must be considered in connection with what he said in his *Poverty of Philosophy,* that:

> In this struggle—a veritable civil war—are united and developed all these elements necessary for a future battle; once having reached this point, association takes on a political character.

Quoting this excerpt from *The Poverty of Philosophy,* Lenin added:

Here we have the programme and the tactics of the economic struggle and the trade union movement for several decades to come, for the whole long period in which the workers are preparing for a "future battle." [1]

Marx, basing himself on the subordination of the economic struggle to the political struggle of the working class, came to the conclusion that the strike was one of the important and effective forms of the struggle. Bakunin, starting from his theory of rejecting politics, drew the conclusion that the strike was the *only* form of struggle. And what Bakunin mapped out, his adherents afterwards developed into a confused theory and tactic, the catastrophic consequences of which particularly affected, and still affect, the labour movement in the Latin countries. With Marx there was complete unity between theory and practice. With Bakunin and his adherents, theory and practice were independent of one another in all fields including the field of the strike movement. On this point the pamphlet written by Engels, *The Bakuninists at Work,* is very interesting and of value even to-day.

Engels' pamphlet is devoted to the tactics of the Bakuninists in the Spanish revolution of 1873. With regard to the slogan raised by the adherents of Bakunin calling for the general strike, Engels wrote that as far back as 1839 the Chartists had preached the "holy month," *i.e.,* a strike of the workers all over England. Analysing step by step the tactics of the Bakuninists in that Spanish revolution, Engels finds that:

(1) The Bakuninists in Barcelona had recourse to the general strike in order to refrain from a revolt on this pretext. (2) Instead of overthrowing the state, they attempted to create numerous small states. (3) The Bakuninists rejected their principle that the workers must not take part in any revolution that does not aim at the immediate and complete emancipation of the working class. (4) By joining the government committees formed in the different towns they violated their dogma that a revolutionary government is a new betrayal. (5) Being opposed, in words, to politics, they, in deeds, supported the bourgeois party,

[1] Lenin, "Kary Marx," *Collected Works,* Vol. XVIII, p. 44. (Italics mine.—*A.L.*). *The Teachings of Karl Marx,* No. 1 Little Lenin Library, p. 34.

which politically exploited the workers and kicked them into the bargain.

Engels concludes: "In a word, the Bakuninists set an excellent example of how revolutions ought not to be made."

What Engels wrote about 1874 was repeated on a broader scale during the Spanish revolution of 1931-32. Bakuninism hinders and sabotages the development of the revolution in Spain.

From the theory, policy and tactics of Marx and Bakunin, we see that strike tactics are not something divorced from general lines of principle. It means that the revolutionary Marxists have their own strike tactics—differing radically from the strike tactics of the anarchists and reformists. The economic and political battles developing in the capitalist countries have reproduced and enlightened anew the chief differences of the past under present conditions. Life and struggle have confirmed the correctness of the Marxian positions concerning the organic connection and close interweaving of the economic and the political struggle of the working class.

Life has shown that he who does not link up the struggle for the workers' demands with the final goal, and *vice versa,* sabotages the struggle for the liberation of the working class, whether he wants to do so or not, and plays into the hands of the bourgeoisie.

CHAPTER IX

Pseudo-Marxists and the Trade Union Critics of Marx

WHAT is the chief difference between Marxism and the pre-Marxist and near-Marxist theories? What is the main difference between Marxism and pseudo-Marxism? This difference was defined by Lenin in his famous work *State and Revolution*. Here Lenin writes:

> Only he is a Marxist who *extends* the acceptance of the class struggle to the acceptance of the *dictatorship of the proletariat*. Herein lies the most profound difference between a Marxist and a mediocre petty (and also—big) bourgeois. On this touchstone a *real* understanding and acceptance of Marxism must be tested.[1]

If this is the angle from which we consider the critics of Marx hailing from the trade union camp, we see that precisely the dictatorship of the proletariat was the stumbling-block for all open and concealed enemies of revolutionary Marxism. This does not mean that they tried seriously, on the basis of actual data, to deny this corner-stone of the teachings of Marx. No, the trade union critics of Marx at first passed by this question, leaving this task to the "pure politicians." What went on in the heads of many trade unionists was formulated by Eduard Bernstein, the real spiritual father of social-fascism. Bernstein, as early as 1899, came out with his *Prerequisites of Socialism,* which should be duly dubbed the holy book of modern Social-Democracy. In this book of Bernstein's we find both industrial democracy, the growing into socialism by means of social reforms, and the democratisation of industry through the medium of the trade unions, etc. Bern-

[1] Lenin, *State and Revolution. Collected Works* (Russian edition), Vol. XXI, p. 392.

stein, in writing his book, leaned for support on the trade unions, while the trade unionists, turning more and more away from Marx, became encouraged and openly recognised Bernstein as their theoretician and leader.

Before Bernstein published his book the trade union pseudo-Marxists concealed their disagreement with Marx; but after the publication of the book, it became the fashion among the leaders of the German trade unions to "criticise" Marx. The trade unions in most cases did not theorise: they simply revised Marx in their day-to-day work, they distorted his teachings in practice and turned the elementals of Marxism on the *rôle* of the trade unions under the capitalist State upside down. If we examine historically the development of the anti-Marxian views of the trade unionists, we see that on the following questions they pursued the following lines:

(1) The theory of the class struggle "is, itself," correct; however, it loses its significance with the development of the trade unions and the establishment of democracy; (2) Revolution is an obsolete conception, it corresponds to a lower level of social development; the democratic State precludes revolutions and the revolutionary struggle; (3) Democracy assures the working class the peaceful passing over from capitalism to socialism, and therefore the dictatorship of the proletariat is not and cannot be on the order of the day; (4) The theory of impoverishment held good at one time, but now it has become obsolete; (5) During the epoch of Marx it was perhaps true that the leading *rôle* in the trade unions belonged to the party. But to-day, only party-political neutrality can ensure the effective development of the trade union movement; (6) During the epoch of Marx strikes had to be considered perhaps as one of the most important weapons of struggle, but now the trade unions have outgrown this, etc.

Thus, everything led to the point that Marxism had become out of date, that it must be re-examined, corrected and supplemented. The work of "correcting" Marxism was divided between the Social-Democrats and the trade unions. Before the war this was done under the slogan of the necessity of "enriching and devoloping Marxism on the basis of the theories of Marx."

The German and Austrian varieties were considered the most Marxist trade union movements. For many years they made use of Marx's name. However, they did with Marx just what German Social-Democracy had done. About this Lenin eloquently writes the following:

> What is now happening to Marx's doctrine has, in the course of history, often happened to the doctrines of other revolutionary thinkers and leaders of oppressed classes struggling for emancipation. During the lifetimes of great revolutionaries, the oppressing classes have visited relentless persecution on them and received their teaching with the most savage hostility, the most furious hatred, the most ruthless campaign of lies and slanders. After their death, attempts are made to turn them into harmless icons, canonise them, and surround their names with a certain halo for the "consolation" of the oppressed classes and with the object of duping them, while at the same time emasculating and vulgarising the real essence of their revolutionary theories and blunting their revolutionary edge. At the present time the bourgeoisie and the opportunists within the labour movement are co-operating in this work of adulterating Marxism. They omit, obliterate and distort the revolutionary side of its teachings, its revolutionary soul. They push to the foreground and extol what is or seems acceptable to the bourgeoisie. All the social-chauvinists are now "Marxists"—joking aside! And more and more do German bourgeois professors, erstwhile specialists in the demolition of Marx, speak now of the 'national-German' Marx, who, they aver, has educated the labour unions which are so splendidly organised for conducting a predatory war.[1]

The trade unionists of Germany outwardly paid homage to Marx, at the time when the whole theory and practice of the trade union movement of Germany was diametrically opposed to the theory and practice of Marx. The more powerful German capitalism grew, the more rapidly its influence spread over new markets, the more rapid was the ideological rapprochement between German capitalists and the leaders of the German trade union movement. It will suffice to recollect the action of the trade unions of Germany in 1905 against a May First Strike, against political strikes, for neutrality of the trade unions, and generally the actions of the German trade unions during the course of many years against every attempt to raise concretely the question

[1] Lenin, *State and Revolution*, Chapter I. Martin Lawrence, London.

of the struggle against war; it will suffice to remember the imperialist tendencies which, even prior to the war, had been openly manifested both in the ranks of the Social-Democratic Party and the trade unions, to draw the conclusion that for the Free Trade Unions of Germany Marxism served only as a sign-board.

The war exposed precisely what the pseudo-Marxists had tried to conceal. Whereas Marx, in 1848, wrote that "the working men have no country," that no one "can take from them what they have not got," [1] the German "Marxists" found their fatherland in imperialist Germany and became agitators and organisers of the working masses to speed on the victory of this imperialist fatherland, became the ideological purveyors of cannon fodder for the front.

Marx spoke and wrote about the class struggle. He devoted his life to turning the working class into a class for itself, to wresting the working class away from the bourgeoisie. The German "Marxists" replaced the class struggle by class collaboration, created a whole theory about "participation in the management of capitalist economy."

> It will be the task of the trade unions [writes Nestriepke, an apologist of the German reformist trade union movement] to demand as a matter of principle that the factory workers and office employees working at the enterprise concerned be given the right to participate in determining questions of employing and discharging workers, this through corresponding regulations, through schooling, influencing individual workers and the factory workers. At the same time they must also see to it that there be no abuse of the right to participate in the management which will impair the profitableness of the enterprise and will injure the real tasks of the enterprise.[2]

The trade unions therefore are turned into custodians of capitalist surplus value under the guise of the "participation of the workers in the economic and technical management of the enterprises."

---

[1] *Communist Manifesto.* Martin Lawrence, p. 26.
[2] S. Nestripke: *The Trade Union Movement,* Stuttgart, 1923, Vol. I, p. 44.

All the teachings of Marx on the class struggle, that the trade unions are organs of struggle against capital, have been replaced by the theory of industrial and economic democracy and equality between Labour and Capital, allowing private ownership of the means of production to remain in the hands of the capitalists. If the working class "participates" in organising the national economy, it will be interested in preserving the capitalist economy, and in defending it against destructive forces. This is how the trade unions become allies of the bourgeoisie, by suppressing the revolutionary labour movement, by suppressing all who revolt against the power of Capital.

While Marx raised the question of the dictatorship of the proletariat, the German "Marxists" for many years have tried and are trying to prove that the dictatorship of the proletariat is an invention of Moscow and that the only form of government acceptable to the trade unions is bourgeois democracy. While Marx proved that the State was a weapon of oppression of one class by another, the Austro-German "Marxists" who headed the trade unions of these countries have been trying to prove that the democratic State stands above classes, that it is and in future will be the arbiter in the conflicts between Capital and Labour.

Marx proved that only by obdurate combat, by developing all forms of struggle, especially strikes, will the proletariat be able to gain something from the bourgeoisie. The German "Marxists" argue that this theory has become out-of-date, that "strikes are always risky," that "strike calls are much more dangerous [for whom?—A. L.] in a country where modern industry is developed, with its large-scale enterprises, employers' associations, etc."; that "the zest for struggle among the modern trade unions [read "among the trade union bureaucrats."—A. L.], acting in conditions of present-day developed economy, will be considerably less," that "the economic struggle in a developed system of economy is in the first instance built on negotiating, probing and waiting tactics," [1] and, finally, this pearl of pearls, taken from the tactical arsenal of Legien:

The more careful an organisation is in putting forward new demands, the more categorically it fights for these demands and

[1] Nestriepke, *The Trade Union Movement*, Stuttgart, 1923, Vol I, p. 96.

the less frequently it applies the extreme measure of strikes, *the sooner it will succeed in winning victories even without a struggle.*[1]

Thus, it appears that Marx was wrong when he considered that the working class would not be able to win anything without a struggle. Nestriepke, together with the loyal German trade unionists, rejects all of this. They, mind you, are anxious to win victories without struggle! The famous military writer Clausewitz wrote that "no equivalent can replace a battle." But the German trade unionists have invented a new method of *trying to win victories* [for whom?—A. L.] without a struggle. He who doubts the miraculous results of this tactic (victory without a struggle!) should look into the history of Germany and he will convince himself that fourteen years of such "victories" have led to Hitler.

In order to see clearly where these "Marxists" landed, let us give a few more examples. At the Hamburg Congress of the German trade unions (1928), the official speaker, Naphtali, solemnly declared that the "trade union movement has succeeded in opposing and overcoming the decisive capitalist tendency towards impoverishment" and that "we now witness an upsurge of the working class." Tarnov, the theoretician of the A.D.G.B. (All German Trade Union Federation), said:

> We are realistic statesmen. Our line differs from the old viewpoint which used to dominate the labour movement and which was able to dominate there precisely because the once correct viewpoint of the tendency of capitalism has to-day become petrified (!) *ideology*. The old position [that is the position of Marx.— A. L.] was essentially a stand of resignedness. . . . We are instilling into the working masses more optimistic views . . . than those formerly held on the condition of the workers.[2]

Indeed, Tarnov is even "better" than Nestriepke. The old conception of Marx was: fight and you will win something. The new conception states: don't fight, wait, and you will get much

[1] Minutes of the Thirteenth Congress of German Trade Unions, 1928, p. 11.
[2] *Ibid.*, p. 210.

more. Finally, in order to "crown the edifice," let us give one more dictum from Tarnov's book, *Why Be Poor?*

> Poverty is no economic necessity, but a social ailment, which doubtlessly can be cured even within the framework of capitalist economy.

Exactly! Why be poor if it is possible to go over to the side of the bourgeoisie and live in clover. Tarnov's book and its contents remind one of the American advertisements, "Why Have Corns?", in which the honourable public is informed that this ailment can be cured "within the framework of the capitalist order" for fifty cents. The A.D.G.B. has a great many of these corn-cure theoreticians, each of whom has solved the problem of poverty for himself.

In the circles of the reformist trade union bureaucrats in Germany an anecdote is told which Professor Erik Noelting related amid friendly laughter at a congress of the wood-workers of Germany. "The Swedish political-economist Sven Hollander once came to Germany for the purpose of visiting the house in Treves where Karl Marx was born. To his great surprise, in Marx's home town, not one of the passers-by could tell him where that house was. Roving through the streets he found a house which had a red flag; he thought that this surely must be the house in which Karl Marx was born, all the more so since there was a sign on it with the inscription, "Trade Union House of Treves." When he entered, one of the employees informed him: "No, this is not the house where Marx was born; this is the trade union house. *The house where Marx was born is too small for the trade unions;* it is situated not far from here."

Having told this "interesting" anecdote, Professor Noelting commented on it in the following words:

> This anecdote excellently shows the close proximity which even to-day exists between the trade unions and the teachings of Marx. On the other hand, it shows that the trade unions were compelled to go beyond Marx. . . . There is a transitional stage between capitalism and socialism which I believe is characterised by three features: politically—*by coalition governments,* juridically—*by labour rights,* economically—*by industrial and economic democracy.* The trade unions in all of their actions

logically presuppose that capitalism has *elastic walls,* and that under the conditions of capitalism a considerable improvement and a rise to a higher level are possible.[1]

Now everything is clear. They have "gone beyond" Marx. The house of Marx was too small for the German trade union bureaucrats. Indeed! The house of Stinnes, this "go-getter" of a business man who grew fat on the war and speculation, is much bigger. It is not an accident that Stinnes called one of his steamers *Karl Legien,* for many years the leader of the reformist trade union movement of Germany. The house of Hindenburg, Brüning and Hitler is much bigger. It is not an accident that Leipart, President of the A.D.G.B., offered his services as a lackey in this "rich man's house." The home of Borsig, President of the Manufacturers' Association of Germany, is much bigger, and so Herr Leipart sent a telegram of condolence to the Manufacturers' Association on the occasion of the death of Borsig, this "noble man." If all this is "Marxism," then what is shameless infamy and treachery? How can this complete renunciation of the most elementary principles of the labour movement be explained? By fear of the masses, fear of the revolution. This fear of the masses which overwhelms the German trade union bureaucrats came to haunt them particularly after Hitler came to power. The bulk of the membership was perturbed, they demanded a united front with the Communists. But what did the A.D.G.B. do, while it still had millions of workers in its ranks? On February 20, 1933, it forwarded a letter to Hindenburg in which these "labour leaders" implored the Field Marshal to take a stand in defence of the workers. This complaint stated in part:

We appeal to you as President of the German Reich, to you who are in duty bound and are willing to protect the constitution. We appeal to you, as the German organisation in whose ranks the major part of those who fought at the front are united. These millions, among whom there are adherents of the most diverse political parties, did not fight and shed their blood for Germany during the World War to let responsible German authorities tell them fifteen years later that they do not belong to

[1] All of these quotations have been taken by me from F. David: *Der Bankrott des Reformismus (Bankruptcy of Reformism).*

K

the forces that are building the state, that they are not a part of the nation's population. No one in Germany has so exalted a position that he may dare charaterise the World War veterans—regardless of the political party to which he may belong—and their organisations as second-rate Germans. . . .

We hope and trust that you, Mr. President, the military leader during the World War, will take action with all the means at your disposal against this dishonour done to millions of those who fought at the front.[1]

This entreaty represents the most shameful document ever issued even by the German reformist trade unions. First of all, to complain to Hindenburg about Hitler is like complaining about the devil to his grandmother, and then the idea of parading their military-patriotic merits as an argument against the fascist raids creates a pitiful impression, indeed. This is how the "Marxist" leaders of the German trade unions descended from one capitulation to another, and finally knelt grovelling before the very feet of General Hindenburg.

How can all of this be explained? *By fear of the masses, fear of the revolution.*

Lassalle once said about the progressive party of his period: "Its principal and basic rule is *anything but revolution from below, better despotism from above.*" [2] This "principal and basic rule" is also the line adhered to by the "Marxists" of the Second and Amsterdam Internationals.

While German and Austrian Marxists sabotaged the teachings of Marx, passing from quiet methods to open and bolder attacks, flaunting their Marxist frocks by force of tradition, anarchism and the revolutionary syndicalism which it bred waged an open war against Marx and his teachings. The anarchists and anarcho-syndicalists claimed that the opportunist actions of the German, French and other socialists were the result of their Marxist view-point. Opportunism and revisionism were represented to the masses as Marxism. This criticism from the "Left" and the bitter

---

[1] *Vossische Zeitung*, February 22, 1933, afternoon edition.
[2] See Franz Mehring, *History of German Social-Democracy*, Vol. II, Dietz, Stuttgart, 1898, p. 88. Mehring wrote: "They preferred to make a bargain with His Royal Highness rather than grant the workers a share of the victor's booty." (p. 370.)

experiences of the opportunist policy of the Socialist parties in the Latin countries (France, Spain) caused some sections of the workers to have no confidence in Marxism generally. Among the critics of Marxism there was one group in France which tried to "purge" Marx and turn him into a theoretician of the anarcho-syndicalist trade union movement. Attempts to associate Marx with anarcho-syndicalism were made by Lagardelle, Sorel, Bert, Arturo Labriola, Leon, etc. In his book, *La décomposition du Marxisme,* George Sorel, the most talented of them, declares that he wants to take the Marxism of Marx, but not of his commentators of the type of Bernstein, etc. Such a line could have been welcomed if, while writing a correct but inadequate criticism of Bernstein, he had not turned Marx into a sort of Proudhon. Here is what Sorel writes:

One might say about Marxism that it is a "philosophy of the hands" and not a "philosophy of the brain," considering that it aims only at one thing—to convince the working class that the whole of its future depends upon the class struggle; Marxism wants to lead it along the path on which it, while organising for the struggle, will be able to find ways and means of getting along without *entrepreneurs.* . . . On the other hand, Marxism must not be confused with political parties, even with the most revolutionary, for the latter are forced to function as bourgeois parties, to change their position in dependence upon election considerations, and when necessary to make compromise with other groups which have a similar electorate; whereas Marxism is invariably imbued solely with thought for absolute revolution.

Several years ago it seemed as if the time for Marxism had passed, and that it, together with many other philosophies, would now take its place in the necropolis of deceased gods. Only an historic impulse could restore it to life; for this end it was necessary that the proletariat organise with purely revolutionary intentions, *i.e.,* that it completely dissociate itself from the bourgeoisie. . . .

. . . And now it turned out that the learned doctors of Marxism felt lost in the face of an organisation, built on the principle of the class struggle, interpreted in the strictest sense of the word [he refers to syndicates.—*A. L.*]. In order to find a way out of the quandary, these doctors indignantly spoke of a new attack of the anarchists, in view of the fact that many of the anarchists, on the advice of Pelloutier, had joined the trade unions and the labour exchanges. . . .

The 'New School' . . . did not claim it was creating a new party, which would compete with the others for their working-class adherents. Its aspiration was a different one. It was to understand the nature of the movement, which seemed unintelligible to all. It took an altogether different road from that of Bernstein; little by little it rejected all formulas, those of utopianism and those of Blanquism, and thus purged traditional Marxism of all that was not properly Marxian and aimed to preserve only that which comprised, in its opinion, the core of this doctrine, only that which assures the glory of Marx.

The theory of catastrophe (which scandalises the socialists who desire to combine Marxism with the practices of democratic politicians) is absolutely compatible with the general strike, which for the revolutionary syndicalists marks the advent of the future society.[1]

This is all the criticism from the "Left." True that Marxism cannot be confused with parliamentarianism; true that according to Marxism the future depends upon the class struggle (not upon the conception but upon the struggle!), but it is thrice wrong to say that the fact that the anarchists are joining the trade unions, that anarcho-syndicalist theory and practice are being created, assures the glory of Marx; it is wrong to say that Marx's theory of catastrophe (*Zusammenbruchstheorie*) and the anarchist general strike, are one and the same. Marx speaks about the struggle for power, about the establishment of the dictatorship of the proletariat, but the anarchists and anarcho-syndicalists have partly consciously and partly unconsciously overlooked this real revolutionary theory of Marxism and criticised its falsification instead of Marxism: what Sorel calls the disintegration of Marxism is the disintegration of the critics of Marx. The attempts of Sorel to pour some anarcho-syndicalist blood into the veins of Marxism have failed. Neo-Marxism proved to be no more than an electrical hash. The fact is that Sorel and his pupils have not understood the essence of Marx's teachings, have not understood the question of the dictatorship of the proletariat raised by Marx.

[1] G. Sorel, *La Décomposition du Marxisme,* Paris, 1907.

What brought revolutionary syndicalism closer to revolutionary Marxism? The protest against parliamentary cretinism, the protest against collaboration with the bourgeoisie. What conclusions did revolutionary syndicalism draw from this? That the main evil lies in the State and parliamentary elections, and that if we refuse to participate in parliamentary elections, and reject all dictatorship, the problem is settled. What conclusions did revolutionary Marxism draw? It considered it necessary to utilise Parliament and parliamentary elections, in a real revolutionary, Bolshevik manner, to destroy the bourgeois State and establish the dictatorship of the proletariat for the entire transition period. By rejecting political action, Sorel denied the necessity of a political party of the proletariat and came to the essential anarcho-syndicalist thesis: the trade union is sufficient unto itself. Rejecting the State and the necessity of the dictatorship of the proletariat, Sorel came to reject also the armed uprising; in the place of uprising he called for the strike with "folded arms." Not understanding the course and tendency of the development of capitalism, Sorel created the theory of "social peace": he denies the necessity of violence, thus filling in the gap of his theory. His companions-in-arms and pupils, screening themselves behind "Left" phrases, preached reformist ideas. "The revolution," Arturo Labriola writes, "issues from the womb of the economic process itself, from consecutive changes." Lagardelle intends to replace "capitalist right" with new right within the framework of capitalist society, while Edward Bert sees in Proudhon, just as in Marx, the "theoretical forerunner" of revolutionary syndicalism. We have seen how Marx "combined" his theories with those of Proudhon. The synthesis of the proletarian theories of Marx and the petty-bourgeois theory of Proudhon could not but lead to theoretical confusion and a politically incorrect line. We see the same in pre-war French anarcho-syndicalism. Anarcho-syndicalism, disporting itself in the gay-coloured frocks of "terrifying Leftism," during the imperialist war followed the socialist and trade union internationals, followed the war chariot of imperialism. This is how the ideological and political communion of ideas between the "Right" and "Left" revisionists of Marx was proved. The honour of Marxism and the international labour movement was saved not by the much-vaunted revolutionariness of the anarcho-syndicalists, but by Bolshevism, which "was raised on the granite base of Marxism" (Lenin).

History has made it possible for us to test in the crucible of revolutionary experience: revolutionary Marxism (U.S.S.R.), reformism (Germany) and anarcho-syndicalism (Spain). Here are three revolutions in which it was possible, on the basis of experience, to test the correctness of their theories and policies. We know that the U.S.S.R. victoriously completed its first Five-Year Plan, thanks to the consistent application of revolutionary-Marxist, Bolshevik policy. We know that fourteen years of social-democratic policy have reduced the proletariat of Germany to unheard-of misery, to the bloody reign of the fascist baton, to a terrific offensive against the working class. Finally, we know that the anarcho-syndicalists of Spain, who led considerable sections of the Spanish proletarian masses, are leading the working class of that country from one defeat to another, that part of the anarcho-syndicalists openly supports the bourgeois republic, while another part, by its policy, splits the workers' ranks, and by refusing to prepare the masses for the struggle for power through Soviets, facilitates the task of the Spanish bourgeoisie of brutally suppressing the workers' and peasants' movement. Such are the facts, facts that are stubborn, indisputable. What is the value, then, of the lamentations against Marxism uttered by the central organ of the anarcho-syndicalist National Confederation of Labour in Spain, the *Solidaridad Obrera?* Here is what this paper writes:

> Social-Democracy, called to-day social-fascism by its Communist sons, is the specific product of Marxism; Communism, whether it likes it or not, is the legitimate son of this social-fascism. They are twins to such an extent that in those places where the Social-Democrats apply revolutionary phraseology, as in Austria, for example, Communism cannot exist because it is deprived of its basis, of its phrases.[1]

This is how far this dexterous anarchist went. The Social-Democrats are Marxists, the Communists are Marxists, consequently the Communists and Social-Democrats are one and the

---

[1] The author of this article is Orabon, one of the leaders of the Anarchist Federation of the Iberian Peninsula.

same. This argument reminds one of the famous "mathematical" formula that "the half-dead are equal to the half-alive, consequently, the dead are equal to the living." No, Sr. Orabon, even in Spain you will not succeed in mixing up in one heap those who stand on opposite sides of the barricades, you will not succeed in throwing on to one heap the revolutionary Marxists and the reformists, who fight one another in armed conflict. You had better prove, not in words, but in deeds, that you really know how to defeat the bourgeoisie. You claim that the "dictatorship of the proletariat really means only one more oligarchy"; your friend Chelso in this same paper expresses surprise that "our brothers in their liberation struggle base themselves upon the low and artificial ideology of dogmatic, out-of-date Marxism"; Maxim Libert also in the same paper informs the Spanish workers of the "influence of Red imperialism, created under the fire of Bolshevik sham revolutionariness," and that "there is no marked difference between the Caesarean conception of the king (Louis XIV) and the State Jacobinism of the Soviet dictator (Lenin)."

What can be said about this invective against Bolshevism? Only one thing—that the anarchists see no difference between a dictatorship that shoots landlords and capitalists and a dictatorship that shoots workers. Inasmuch as the anarcho-syndicalists in their attacks upon the Comintern and the R.I.L.U. chiefly come out against the dictatorship of the proletariat, or, as this same Libert calls it, "the drill-ground dictatorship," we again raise the question: why have the anarcho-syndicalists, who lay claim to the title of revolutionaries, not been able to deal one serious blow to the Spanish bourgeoisie, despite the absolutely splendid heroism, extraordinary self-sacrifice and exemplary militancy of the Spanish proletariat? One can spout from morning to night against Marxism, without being in the least convincing. *We know why this happened and we will strain every effort in order to make this known to every Spanish worker.* We shall explain to the Spanish workers that not only the reformists but also the Anarcho-Syndicalists are responible for their defeats. How can they defeat the bourgeoisie, if people in the central organ of the National Confederation of Labour express "profound" ideas like the following:

The fractions of State socialism, as is the case in Russia to-day, desire to consolidate political power, in order afterwards to destroy it again, according to their own statements. Anarchism, on the contrary, smashes it and scatters it despite the green revolutionaries who took up philosophy in the universities of Moscow; without such preliminary precedent the present social revolution will be impossible. An unbridgeable abyss exists between the revolution fought for by the parties (*i.e.*, the Communist Party) and that which the National Confederation of Labour aims at. Ours belongs to the present, while the revolution of State socialism belongs to the past. With the Russian revolution the cycle of party revolutions has ended.[1]

If a revolution of the type of the October Revolution is the last, what kind of a revolution do the Anarcho-Syndicalists of Spain promise to the international proletariat? Do they think that the German proletariat in its struggle against Hitler must not take lessons from the Bolsheviks, who have smashed their bourgeoisie, but must take their lessons from the anarchists, who are leading the proletariat from one defeat to another? Must the proletariat follow the legacy of the Paris Commune, create a new type of State and do just what the Bolsheviks have been doing ever since 1917 until this day, or should it follow the example of the Bakuninists of 1873 and of the Anarcho-Syndicalists of 1931-33? What makes the anarchists believe that the workers in the capitalist countries will prefer defeat to victory? There really is an impassable gulf between such viewpoints and communism, but there is no gulf between the anarchist workers and communism. Of this fact the anarchist leaders are convincing themselves in practice, as they are daily losing influence over great sections of workers who have followed them heretofore. We shall have to dwell also on the joint attack by the reformists and Anarcho-Syndicalists of all shades and colours upon the leading *rôle* of the Party in the trade union movement, and the effort to use the name of Karl Marx for these ends. For the last sixty years the Anarcho-Syndicalists and reformists have been arguing that Marx advocated neutrality. The occasion for this was an alleged interview given by Marx to Haman, a

[1] *Solidaridad Obrera,* November 16, 1932.

metal worker of Hanover, who in 1869 published the following concerning this pretended "interview":

> If the trade unions really want to accomplish their task, they must never associate themselves with any political unions or become dependent upon them in any way. If they do, it deals them a death blow. The trade unions are schools of socialism. In the trade unions the workers are trained to become socialists. Because there the daily struggle against capitalism takes place before their eyes. All political parties, no matter which, without exception enthuse the working masses only transiently, for a certain period of time. But the trade unions on the contrary form permanent contacts with the masses of workers; they can only really be a working-class party and act as a bulwark against the power of capital. The largest sections of the workers, regardless of party affiliation, have already come to the conclusion that the material conditions of the proletariat must be improved. Moreover, if the material conditions of the workers improve, they will be able to pay more attention to the upbringing of their children; their wives and children will not have to go to the factory; they will be able to care better for their own mental and physical training and will become socialists without being aware of it.[1]

This interview was doubtless "doctored" by Haman, for it contains a number of formulations absolutely different from anything Marx ever said or wrote during his whole life, and Marx was not one of those who write one thing and say another. Marx could not have said that "all political parties, *no matter which,* attract the working masses only for a certain period of time." Then what was Haman's scheme? Haman, interested evidently in the "independence" of the trade unions, "doctored" the original text by deleting Marx's statement that this referred to *bourgeois* parties only, thus giving an altogether different political meaning to the statement and turning Marx into an "Independent."

That this is so can be seen from the fact that Haman formulated the question he put to Marx as follows:

> Must the trade unions depend mostly upon the political *Verein* (union), if they want to be able to exist?

[1] Marx, *Value, Price and Profit* (Appendix to German edition) p. 78.

From the way he put the question one can see what kind of an answer he wanted to get. This is why we have every reason to believe that Haman himself had so "edited" the interview that it acquired the content he desired. It is only strange that a Bolshevik Party such as the Communist Party of Germany should publish this interview in the form of a supplement to a popular edition of the basic works of Marx *without any commentary whatsoever*.

Thus Marx was turned into an "Independent."

> That is why the opportunist theory of the "independence" and "neutrality" of the non-Party organisations, which theory is the progenitor of *independent* parliamentarians and publicists who are *isolated* from the Party, and of *narrow-minded* trade unionists and co-operative society officials who have become petty bourgeois, is wholly incompatible with the theory and practice of Leninism.[1]

This is what revolutionary Marxism means by "independence" of the trade union movement. But the reformists and adherents of the theory of independence of the trade union movement in all countries stick to the falsified text, in order to prevent Bolshevism from penetrating the masses of organised and unorganised workers. All the practical and theoretical leaders of the reformist and Anarcho-Syndicalist trade union movement try to prove that they, "according to Marx," ought to be independent of socialism, *i.e.*, be dependent on capitalism. Hermann Müller, when quoting this interview, triumphantly declared: "Marx thus stood for strict neutrality of the trade unions."[2] This unanimity of all anarcho-reformists, of all enemies of revolutionary Marxism alone must impel us to be on the alert and attentively examine just what doctoring has been done in this interview.

However, Marxism is too firm to be easily exploded by such distortions of Marx. This attempt, just like all others, failed miserably.

The extent to which this falsified quotation was seriously believed can be seen from the fact that so prominent a man as

[1] Stalin, *Foundations of Leninism*, Moscow, 1934 (English edition), p. 94.
[2] Hermann Müller, *Karl Marx and the Trade Unions* (German edition), 1921, p. 73.

Daniel De Leon referred to this quotation of Marx in support of his development of the theory of the primacy of the economic over the political organisation. De Leon said that the conclusions to be drawn from these words of Marx are:

(1) . . . That a true political party of labour is bound to carry into the political arena the sound principles of the revolutionary economic organisation *which it reflects*.

(2) . . . That the revolutionary act of achieving the overthrow of Capitalism and the establishment of Socialism is *the function reserved to the economic organisation*.

(3) . . . That the 'physical force' called for by the revolutionary act *lies inherent in the economic organisations*.

(4) . . . That the element of 'force' consists, not in a military or other organisation implying violence, but in the *structure* of the economic organisation.

(5) . . . That the economic organisation is not 'transitory' but is the present *embryo of the future Government of the Republic of Labour*.[1]

Daniel De Leon claims that all of these theses are the result of the interview that Marx gave to Haman. Even if Marx had really said what is ascribed to him by Haman, it would still have been impossible to draw the conclusions that De Leon drew. Daniel De Leon, this greatest and most revolutionary leader of pre-war American socialism, could not, despite all of his distinguished political, oratorical and literary ability, create a party and head the movement of the masses. Why? Because in the basic problems of party, trade union and class, he had a non-Marxist platform, though he thought that he was a real Marxist. Daniel De Leon clearly saw all the corruption and rottenness of the American Federation of Labour. He was the author of the phrase, "labour lieutenants of capitalism"; it was he who said in 1896 that "the American Federation of Labour is a steamer that never was seaworthy; and now she had run aground and been seized by a pirate crew." It was he who said at the end of the nineteenth century that the leaders of the American Federation of Labour

[1] Daniel De Leon, *Marx as Text*, "Industrial Unionism," New York, 1910. p. 39.

were not the Right wing of the labour movement, but the Left wing of the bourgeoisie. In spite of this, in spite of his good qualities as a revolutionary, he remained the leader of a sect only. The cause lies in his distortions of Marxism, although subjectively he wanted to apply the Marxist theories. This is how a false line revenges itself when applied to the most important problem of the relationship between the party, the trade unions and the class.

The Marxian industrial unions of England represent a rather interesting variety of the combination of Marxism and syndicalist sectarianism. The Marxian unionist in England considered that the trade unions would have to go under, and that the only path towards salvation was the one of creating a new trade union movement in the form of One Big Union, of the type of the Industrial Workers of the World in the United States. During the war and after the October Revolution, semi-Marxist, semi-syndicalist sentiments appeared among the trade unionists, who expressed their sympathies for the Bolsheviks, but themselves thought that the "main thing was the economic organisation and the economic struggle." Marxian unionism turned into industrial unionism, which in its turn was split into two schools. One of them was of the opinion that the "political struggle was necessary in order gradually [!] to undermine the capitalist state régime." The other group considered that "the working class must completely discard the political struggle and concentrate all forces on applying the weapon of the economic struggle." Both of these schools *"base their doctrine upon Marxian economics, upon the materialistic conception of history above all else."* What then is the result of this combination of emasculated Marxism and anarcho-syndicalism? G. D. H. Cole, who reports all these details, states further: "These two tendencies (Marxian unionism and guild socialism) between them never commanded the conscious adherence of more than an infinitesimal fraction of the workers in the trade unions." [1] In view of the fact that infinitesimal fractions refer to mathematics and not to history, we do not intend to dwell on this variety of "Marxists."

[1] G. D. H. Cole, *Introduction to Trade Unionism*, 1924.

So-called theoreticians of all shades and colours wanted to utilise Marx against the Comintern and the Red International of Labour Unions. They "revised" Marxism, "purged" it, "diluted" it with reformist water and anarchist metaphysics, but nothing came of it. Marxism cannot tolerate any alien admixtures and ligatures. Even during Marx's life scores and hundreds of persons tried to refute his theories, to break them into smithereens, but all of these learned men's speculations lived but a day. After each such "refutation" Marx and Marxism rose higher and higher. Fifty years have now elapsed since the death of Marx, but despite these ceaseless "refutations" Marx stands to-day more impregnable than ever, while his assailants have long been forgotten.

As the bourgeoisie could not defeat Marxism by means of a frontal attack, it directed its attack upon Marx and Marxism from within the labour movement. True, this attack caused much harm to the international labour movement; however, in the struggle against these falsifiers, revolutionary Marxism—this integral, monolithic revolutionary doctrine—only gathered strength, became consolidated in consequence.

The question as to who really is the continuer and inheritor of the great cause of Marx is to be determined not by words but by deeds. Were we to judge by words, we should have to recognise as Marxists those who have substituted class collaboration for the class struggle—this basic theory of Marx. We should have to recognise as Marxists Messrs. Kautsky, Stein, Renner, Speyer, Dan, Crispien, Kampfmeyer, etc., if for no other reason than because on the occasion of the fiftieth anniversary of Marx's death they published a symposium entitled: *Marx, der Denker und Kampfer* (*Marx, the Thinker and Fighter*). This book, which besides the title contains nothing of Marxism, represents a fine illustration of how it is possible to turn live, militant and *always up-to-date* Marxism into stone-dead scholastic.[1]

Marxism is not a dogma, but a guide to action. The tasks and tactics of the trade unions are defined as revolutionary action against capitalism.

---

[1] *Marx der Denker und Kämpfer—Gedenksschrift zum 50. Todestag.* Berlin, 1933.

Now if the class struggle has been replaced by class collaboration, if bourgeois democracy is contrasted with proletarian dictatorship, if fascism is "a lesser evil" than communism, then the tasks of the trade unions are one thing. If, however, the class struggle and the establishment of the dictatorship of the proletariat are the guide to action, then the tasks of the trade unions are quite different. With whom, then, is Marx? Is he with the falsifiers of his teachings, or with those who developed the struggle on the basis of his teachings? Where do we find Marxism? In the Amsterdam International, whose leaders sit in the League of Nations, or in the Red International of Labour Unions, thousands of whose members are languishing in capitalist prisons? Who, then, is the continuer of Marx—international reformism, which has become the would-be healer of capitalism, which is doing its utmost to discover some way of salvaging the disintegrating capitalist system, or is it persecuted, oppressed yet ever-victorious communism? This is why we have the right to say to all flunkeys of the bourgeoisie and lackeys of monopolist capital: "Keep your dirty paws off Marx and Marxism!"

CHAPTER X

Marx, the Organiser of the Working Class

THE usual conception of a scientist is that he is cut off from real life. He burrows in books, in historical documents, draws inspiration from his own spirit, allows his thoughts to take flights according to his fancy, unmindful of prosaic life, and creates systems that are destined to correct the blunders of nature. This divorcement from life was cited as proof of the impartiality and true nature of science and its priests who stood above classes. Marx with his scientific and political works shattered the conception of the class impartiality of science and the class neutrality of its bearers. He first of all proved that the highest altitudes of the spirit, barricaded behind exalted and learned words, reflect not only definite social relationships, but also the interests of a definite social class; while on the other hand he proved that the abandonment of the struggle is also a policy, but one favourable to the oppressors and unfavourable to the oppressed.

Marx was a scientist in the best and highest sense of the word. He did not write one line without having first thought it over and verified it dozens of times; he believed that science must serve the struggle, but must not serve to divert the masses from the struggle. He believed that science must sweep away all ideological and political barriers erected in the path of the working class towards its emancipation. Marx excellently understood the historical significance of his scientific work, but "he was a revolutionary first of all" (Engels). He realised that science without revolutionary deeds is as dead as a log. Marx, who discovered the historic mission of the working class, who raised the consciousness and faith of the working class in its own self, considered it necessary to help the working class concretely, to explain his theory to it, to help it organise; and, therefore, he did not stand aloof from the pettiest, day-to-day organisational work, so long as this work concerned the consolidation of the forces of the working class and the interests of socialism.

In 1846 Marx organised the "Committee of Communist Correspondence" and sent a number of letters to the most famous socialists of that period, requesting them to take part in the labours of this committee, hoping in this way to create a unifying centre. On May 5, 1846, Marx wrote to Proudhon:

> The principal aim of our correspondence is meanwhile to set up contacts between the German socialists and the French and English socialists. Thus the social movement in its literary manifestations will advance a step forward to free itself from its national limitation.[1]

We see that this committee formally aimed at mutual information, but in reality there was much more to it. Mutual information exchanged on the level on which the socialist movement stood during the first half of the nineteenth century signified a certain amount of influence exercised by advanced socialism over more backward socialism. Struggle against national limitations—such was the aim of Marx and herein lies the political significance of the Committee of Communist Correspondence. In 1845-46 Marx gave lectures to the workers of Belgium. In 1847 he was the leader of the Communist League, and together with Engels, on the instructions of the League, he drafted the famous *Manifesto of the Communist Party,* which is the basic charter of international communism to this day. The Communist League rapidly developed and gained influence. But the defeat of the revolution in 1848 considerably weakened it. Marx exerted tremendous efforts to preserve and strengthen the organisation, and in a number of documents of an organisational and political character he mapped out a general line for all rank-and-file organisations. In this connection the circular letters of the Central Committee of the Communist League to its organisations are of major importance. In these circular letters we find not only appraisals of the situation but also a number of organisational and tactical

---

[1] Marx to Proudhon, *Die Gesellschaft,* Dietz, Berlin, fourth year, 1927, Vol. II, p. 259.

instructions. The first appeal of the Central Committee of the Communist League, made in March, 1850, declared that the "former organisation of the League has been seriously shattered."[1] The appeal, after comparing the position of the Workers' Party with the democratic party of the petty bourgeoisie, comes to the conclusion that "while the party of the petty bourgeoisie extended its organisations, the Workers' Party has lost its only strong footing." [2] This first appeal also defines the attitude of the revolutionary Workers' Party towards petty-bourgeois democracy.

> The circumstances in which the revolutionary workers' party finds itself, make it go hand in hand with the petty bourgeois democratic party against the faction which it proposes to overthrow, but the party of the workers assumes the attitude of opposition in all matters where the petty bourgeoisie wishes to secure its own position.[3]

This tactical rule goes far beyond the framework of the first half of the nineteenth century. For scores of years it defined the attitude of revolutionary Marxism towards the petty-bourgeois parties. This tactic can be explained by the fact that:

> While the democratic petty bourgeoisie wishes to bring the revolution to as swift a conclusion as possible . . . it is in our interest and it is our task to make the revolution permanent. . . . With us it cannot be a mere matter of a change in the form of private property, but of destroying it as an institution; not in hushing up class antagonism, but in abolishing all classes; not in the improvement of present-day society, but in the foundation of a new society.[4]

What, then, must the workers do when a revolution begins? What demands must they raise and what organisational measures must they undertake in order to direct the course of events in favour of the toilers? In the first place, revolutionaries "must not decry so-called excesses, manifestations of national vengeance, but must assume the leadership of these." Parallel with the demands of bourgeois democracy, the workers must

[1] Marx, Appendix to Engels' *Germany: Revolution and Counter-Revolution*, Martin Lawrence, p. 135.
[2] *Ibid.*, p. 135.   [3] *Ibid.*, p. 138.   [4] *Ibid.*, p. 139.

L

put forward their own demands. They must demand guarantees and compel the new rulers to make "as many concessions and pledges as possible. The surest way is to force them to compromise themselves." [1] Marx wrote:

> They must simultaneously erect their own revolutionary workers' government hard by the new official government whether it be in the form of executive committees, community councils, workers' clubs or workers' committees, so that the bourgeois-democratic government not only will lose its immediate restraint over the workers, but, on the contrary, must at once feel themselves watched over and threatened by an authority behind which stand the mass of the workers. In a word: from the first moment of the victory, and after it, the distrust of the workers must not be directed any more against the conquered reactionary party, but against their previous ally, the petty-bourgeois Democrats, who desire to exploit the common victory only for themselves. [2]

This splendid definition of the tactic to which the workers' party must adhere during a revolution was carried out in practice and verified by experiences during the Russian revolution, where dual power served as the starting-point and the lever for organising the masses and overthrowing the power of the bourgeois and petty-bourgeois parties.

Furthermore, the appeal advises that in case revolutionary events develop, it would become necessary to begin to organise proletarian guards, which must be put at the disposal of the *unions of revolutionary councils (Cf.* "Soviet"—*Ed.*) *elected by the workers:* special attention must be paid to organising the agricultural proletariat. Most important here is "independent position of the party, independent organisation of the party of the proletariat." [3]

These instructions, written over eighty years ago, are astounding because they are still applicable even to-day. This organisational-tactical advice contained the germ of all the subsequent tactics of Bolshevism in three revolutions.

The second appeal of the Central Committee of the Communist League in 1850 gives some information regarding the situation in the Communist League in Belgium, Germany,

Ibid., p. 141.   [2] *Ibid.,* p. 142.   [3] *Ibid.,* p. 146.

Switzerland, France, and England, and again brings up before the weakened local organisations a number of organisational tasks, the principal one of which was work within industrial and agricultural workers' organisations that are under the leadership of hostile elements, for the purpose of winning over the bulk of the members to the side of the revolutionary class struggle. In this same second appeal Marx raised the question of setting up auxiliary non-party organisations:

> With the aid of these broader connections it will be possible to organise our influence very firmly, chiefly our influence upon the peasant unions and the sports societies.

All these instructions aim at rapidly gaining firm ground among the working masses.

How must work be carried on under conditions of permanent repression? Wherever possible—legally; wherever impossible—illegally. Such was the invariable advice given by Marx to his adherents. While being a supporter of illegal Party work, Marx was against hatching conspiracies. Marx strictly differentiated between the one and the other. Marx's reviews of A. Chenu's *Conspirators,* and of L. de la Hodde's *Birth of the Republic in February 1848* [1] are very interesting indeed. Both of these books were published in Paris in 1850. Marx came out strongly against the "alchemists of the revolution" who "improvise revolutions when there are no prerequisites for revolution." [2] These alchemists of the revolution "have a deep contempt for the theoretical education of the workers and for the need to explain to them their class interests." This extreme isolation from the masses leads to the circumstance that the short leap from professional conspirator to the category of paid police spy is such a frequent occurrence.

This characteristic of the alchemists of the revolution was excellently confirmed by the experiences of the Russian anarchists, Maximalists, Social-Revolutionaries and all other parties and groups, which tried to replace mass action by individual acts of a handful of conspirators.

When after the suppression of the revolution of 1848 reaction

[1] *Literary Inheritance,* Vol. III, Dietz, Berlin-Stuttgart, 1923, p. 426.
[2] *Ibid.,* p. 30.

throttled the revolutionary movement in all countries, Karl Marx persistently continued to work on his *Capital* and published a number of political articles in the British, American and German Press on all problems of current politics, maintaining contact at the same time with all of his adherents and doing his best to help in word and in deed. As soon as the labour movement began to show signs of revival after this period of depression, when the workers of various countries again began to express the desire to set up mutual contacts, Marx actively participated in this matter. As a result of trips made by French workers to England, and the consequent fraternisation of French and English workers, the International Workingmen's Association was set up in 1864 and became the prototype of the Third Communist International.

Peter Kropotkin, the apostle of anarchism and patriotic defender of his fatherland during the World War, wrote that the "International was founded without Marx's participation." Kropotkin had reference to the letter which Marx had written to Engels in which he said that he had attended the meeting in the Albert Hall on September 28, 1864, but had merely been a "silent spectator." [1] From this Kropotkin draws the conclusion that Marx had nothing to do with the founding of the International. Peter Kropotkin clearly distorts history, for he concealed from his readers the fact that only thanks to Marx's *preliminary* and *subsequent* work for many years did it become possible for the International to be organised and develop into a powerful force. Furthermore, Marx, in this same letter, relates in detail how he had participated in drafting the *Inaugural Address* and the Statutes, the basic documents of the First International, and how he had succeeded in giving the *Address* and the statutes a theoretically and politically consistent character.

In his letter to Engels dated November 4, 1864, Marx describes in detail the conditions under which the International Workingmen's Association was organised and explains why he went to the meeting in the Albert Hall:

I knew that this time real "powers" were in motion both on the part of Paris as well as London, and therefore I decided to set aside my otherwise standing rule of declining any such invitations.[1]

At this meeting a committee was elected, which in turn elected a sub-committee for drafting a declaration of principles. "Major Wolf," Marx wrote, "proposed that the new Association utilise the statutes of the Italian Workers' societies. This was evidently the work of Mazzini, Weston and Baston. Furthermore, Weston drafted a programme which is full of extraordinary confusion and is indescribably long." These drafts were handed over to Le Lubez, after which a plenary session of the committee was called.

"Inasmuch as Eccarius has written to me that *pericula in mora* (there was danger in delay)," Marx wrote, "I came and was really horrified to hear an abominably phrased, poorly written and absolutely immature preamble read by that chap Le Lubez, pretending to be a declaration of principles. Mazzini could be seen peeping through everywhere, incrustated with the vaguest fragments of French socialism. Besides, it contained the sum and substance of the Italian statutes, which, aside from all the other shortcomings, actually aimed at something totally impossible, a sort of central government (naturally, with Mazzini in the background) of the working class of Europe. I began to oppose gently and after a long talk back and forth, Eccarius proposed that the sub-committee once more re-edit the matter." [2]

Marx firmly resolved not to retain any word of these drafts and when the documents were turned over to him to familiarise himself with them, he deleted all of the old text and composed a Manifesto to the working class, "a sort of review of the adventures of the working class since 1845." [3]

He changed the introduction, dropped the declaration of principles and instead of forty paragraphs in the statutes, he drafted ten.

"All of my proposals," Marx wrote, "were adopted by the sub-committee. I was only charged to incorporate in the preamble to the statutes two 'duty' and 'right' phrases, *i.e.*,

[1] *Ibid.*, p. 196.   [2] *Ibid.*, pp. 197-98.
[3] *Ibid.*, p. 198—Original phrase in English—*Ed.*

'truth, morality and justice.' This, however, is placed so that it
cannot do any harm." [1]

These facts concerning the origin of the first, *basic* documents of the International were not even denied by the
anarchists. They prove that if Marx had not interfered in the
matter, Tolen, Weston and others would have adopted a declaration without socialist content and would have directed the
International Workingmen's Association into other channels.

Here we see that Marx manifested great organisational
ability, forcing all blunderers to renounce their confused programmes and theses. What should be considered more important in founding the International? Solemn speeches delivered
at meetings, or the drafting of the basic document which
actually created this international organisation? Heretofore we
had always thought that Marx, who was formally standing
aside, but who had taken the whole matter into his hands, was
the real founder of the International; the anarchists, however,
will not have it so, for they are more interested in form than in
substance.

Were we to follow Kropotkin, we would conclude that Marx,
generally speaking, had nothing at all to do with the First
International, because he was neither its president nor its secretary. Marx did not attend some of the congresses because he
was busy with his major works. In April 1866, he wrote to Bolte
that he would not go to the congress in Geneva owing to the
fact that he was about to complete his *Capital*. Marx also failed
to attend a number of other congresses, but in spite of this all
basic documents, all basic lines, were mapped out by Marx,
although in some cases non-Marxian formulations found their
way into these documents. Marx believed that if on any subject
the congress adopted the document that had been drafted by
him, this was politically much more important than if he had
made a dozen grandiloquent speeches.

If we accept the version of Kropotkin and his pupils, Marx
and Engels did nothing at all. Cherkezov declared, and this
was repeated by Kropotkin, that Marx and Engels had copied
the *Communist Manifesto* from Considerant. This same Cherkezov—and he is echoed by Kropotkin—went so far as to say

[1] Marx and Engels, *Complete Works* (German edition), Part III, Vol. 3,
pp. 197-98.

that Engels' *The Condition of the Working Class in England* was plagiarised from Bureau, a French journalist. Such is the "objectivism" of the anarchist historians. In their helplessness they vilify Marx, who obdurately and fiercely fought against all verbal revolutionariness and anarchist chatter.

While occupied with his principal works, Marx day after day observed all that was going on throughout the world. In the correspondence between Marx and Engels we find vast material, which bears witness to the exceptionally great and important work done by Marx. He wrote leaflets and appeals, corrected the mistakes of his friends and criticised his allies. He bitterly attacked his enemies, gave advice on how to act in each particular case, dependent upon the situation. Sometimes he was blunt and direct; at other times he expressed his views in a friendly letter. In certain cases he acted through the medium of third persons. Marx always adhered to one major thought— to set up a party of the proletariat on the basis of a revolutionary programme, to clear the minds of at least the vanguard from all ideological confusion which had its roots in the historical past but which hindered the development of the labour movement. Frequently, when Marx had no opportunity to write, Engels would do so upon his advice, in agreement with him or at his, Marx's, initiative. Each day would bring new problems to Marx and Engels; to-day a strike breaks out in Belgium, England or France, to-morrow members of the International are persecuted in France; the day after to-morrow a campaign of vilification is launched against the First International; or they learn of attempts in the United States to form illegal unions, of the refusal of the British trade unions to take part in political struggles, of Proudhonists' and Bakuninists' misdoings, which served to undermine the political and organisational unity of the International; the penetration of alien elements into the workers' organizations; in one place manifestations of "Right" opportunism; elsewhere "Left" sectarianism, etc. Beginning with the organisation of the First International, the labour movement rapidly developed all over the world. Not only correct theoretical lines but also political instructions and organisational advice were necessary. Marx and Engels occupied such an authoritative position in the developing of the labour movement that even had they wanted to they could not have turned a deaf ear to current organisational and tactical problems. In view of the fact that Marx never had any such intention of divorcing himself from the pulsating questions concerning labour, but, on the contrary, took a hand in all programmes, all tactical and organisational problems of the international labour movement, the day-to-day activities of Marx represent a remarkable example of the practical application of revolutionary theory.

Marx could recognise at a distance corruption and hypocrisy in the socialist movement and would not rest until he had achieved some definite results. On October 19, 1877, he wrote to Sorge:

> In Germany a corrupt spirit is raising its ugly head in the ranks of our Party—not so much among the masses as among their leaders.[1]

Marx mercilessly flayed the corrupt spirit in the field of theory, politics and tactics. In the middle of April, 1879, Marx and Engels wrote a circular letter to Bebel, Liebknecht, Bracke and others. This document, aimed at the Zurich trio (Höchberg, Bernstein and Schramm), is a fierce indictment of all forms of opportunism. This trio preached a cautious, prudent attitude towards the bourgeoisie, proposed that Social-Democracy carry on energetic propaganda among the upper strata of society, etc. Here is what Marx and Engels write about these out-pourings:

> They are the representatives of the petty bourgeoisie, who make themselves heard and are full of apprehension that the proletariat, constrained by its revolutionary position, might go too far. Instead of determined political opposition—general mediation; instead of struggle against the government and the bourgeoisie—an attempt to win them over and persuade them; instead of stubborn resistance to maltreatment from above, humble submission and the admission that the punishment is deserved.[2]

Who are they, these capitulators, what is their political origin?

---

[1] *Letters from Becker, Dietzgen, Engels and Marx to Sorge*—Stuttgart, 1921, Dietz, p. 159.
[2] Marx-Engels, *Selected Letters* (German edition) p. 306.

To this question there is an answer in this same circular letter:

> They are the same people who, while giving themselves the appearance of working busily without stop, not only do nothing themselves but seek to prevent anything at all from being done besides chattering; the self-same people who in 1848 and 1849 through their fear of any action hindered the movement at every step and finally caused it to fail; the same people who see a reaction and then are quite astonished to find themselves at last in a blind alley, where neither resistance nor flight is possible; the same people who want to compress history into the scope of their narrow philistine horizon and past whom history proceeds each time to consider the questions on the order of the day. [1]

This brilliant characterisation of the German opportunists bristles with facts of importance for the present. It seems as if it were specially written to characterise German Social-Democracy during the period of Hitler's "Third Reich." This remarkable letter by Marx and Engels ends with the statement that the Party must not keep such gentlemen in its ranks:

> During the course of almost forty years we have stressed the class struggle as the immediate driving force in history, especially the class struggle between the bourgeoisie and the proletariat, as the powerful level of the modern social transformation: therefore we cannot go hand in hand with people who want to delete this class struggle from the movement. On forming the International, we expressly formulated the battle cry: the liberation of the working class must be the work of the working class itself. We consequently cannot go hand in hand with people who openly declare that the workers are too uneducated to liberate themselves, and must be liberated from above at the hands of philanthropic big and petty bourgeois.[2]

This is how the founders of scientific communism taught the leaders of the German Social-Democratic Party. Marx also drew conclusions from his theoretical arguments and therefore this circular letter is a most outstanding organisational and political document of international communism. In this letter we see the great tactical genius of Marx. Step by step he

---

[1] *Ibid.*, p. 307.   [2] *Ibid.*, p. 309.

analyses what opportunism is: he tells us how to struggle against it and draws the corresponding organisational conclusions. Marx, who with great skill drafted the *Inaugural Address* of the First International for the purpose of uniting all the various elements of the labour movement, and who during the foundation of the Workers' Party of France came out in favour of non-Marxian elements joining this Party, was decidedly for a split when he saw that the time for doing so was ripe, when he realised that staying together in one and the same organisation threatened to distort the political line.

"Unity is an excellent thing," wrote Engels to Bebel on October 28, 1882, "as long as it can be maintained, but there are some things of even greater importance than unity." [1]

Marx lashed opportunism, adaptability, subordination of the interests of the working class to those of the bourgeois parties. He attacked alien elements who found their way into socialism, but simultaneously and with no less vigour and passion did he come to grips with "Left" phrasemongers, who dissemble this same opportunism. When the German Communists in the United States, after the International had fallen apart, began to isolate themselves into narrow, sectarian groups, considering it below their dignity to work in reactionary organisations, Engels wrote a letter to Mrs. Wishnevetski, in which he explained that the principal task was to struggle against sectarianism; that work must be carried on in workers' mass organisations and that to isolate ourselves from these labour organisations meant self-isolation from the working class.

"I, therefore," Engels wrote to Mrs. Wishnevetski, "consider the Knights of Labour a very important factor in the movement, which ought not to be pooh-poohed from without but to be revolutionised from within. . . . To expect the Americans to start with the full consciousness of the theory worked out in older industrial countries is to expect the impossible . . . do not make the inevitable confusion of the first start worse confounded by forcing down people's throats things which at present they cannot understand but which they soon will learn." [2]

[1] Marx and Engels, *Selected Letters* (German edition) p. 328.
[2] Engels to Mrs. Wishnevetski, Dec. 28, 1886. Marx-Engels, *Selected Letters*, Moscow, 1933, p. 360.

Several months later Engels again returned to this question and in his letter of January 27, 1887, he wrote to this same Mrs. Wishnevetski:

All our practice has shown that it is indeed possible to colla-borate with the general movement of the working class at every one of its stages without giving up or hiding our own distinct position or even organisation, and I am afraid that if the German-Americans choose a different line they will commit a great mistake.[1]

These tactical instructions of Engels are not out of date even at the present time. They are of live and vital interest and the more one studies the inheritance of Marx and Engels the more one finds organisational and tactical instructions suitable for the present day labour movement.

Marx was at the head of international communism for scores of years. Marx was the mortal enemy of capitalism and there-fore he "was the best hated and most calumniated man of his time" (Engels). But this bothered him least of all. He pursued his chosen path, knowing that this was the path of the best ele-ments of the working class, the path of millions. On October 25, 1881, Engels wrote to Bernstein:

By his theoretical and *practical*[2] work Marx won such a position for himself that the best elements of all the labour move-ments in the various countries have full confidence in him. They come to him for advice in *decisive moments* and as a rule find that his advice is the best. . . . Thus it is not Marx who foists his opinion, not to speak of his will, upon people, but these people themselves come to him of their own accord. It is precisely upon this that Marx's peculiar influence, so extremely important for the movement, is based.[3]

It did not fall to Marx's lot to live and see the triumph of Marxism on one-sixth of the globe's surface, but he knew that the victory of the working class was bound to come and he tirelessly, without a moment's rest, prepared the working class politically

[1] Engels to Mrs. Wishnevetski, Jan. 27, 1887, *Ibid.*, p. 361.
[2] Italics mine.—*A.L.*
[3] Letters from Engels to E. Bernstein—Berlin, Dietz (German edition), 1925, pp. 34-5.

and organisationally for the overthrow of the bourgeoisie. It is therefore ludicrous to observe the attempts of the social-fascist theoreticians to prove that Marx would have sided with them. Of all such attempts, perhaps the most ridiculous was the article written by Woodburn, one of the theoreticians of the British Labour Party. It was entitled, *Would Marx have joined the Labour Party?* Mr. Woodburn replies to this question in the affirmative, for the *Communist Manifesto* coincides with the present programme of the Labour Party. [1] Marx—a Labourist? Indeed, there is no limit to social-fascist cynicism.

The enemies of revolutionary Marxism, desiring to undermine the authority of Marx among the masses, have time and again maliciously emphasised the mistakes made by Marx and Engels in defining the degree of maturity of the revolutionary process. As early as 1907 Lenin replied to all of these wiseacres and prophets:

> Yes, Marx and Engels did err quite often in determining the proximity of the revolution and in their hopes for the victory of the revolution. . . . But *such* mistakes of these giants of revolutionary thought, who were raising and did raise the proletariat of the whole world above the level of petty, everyday, penny-by-penny tasks, are a thousand times more thankful, more magnificent and *historically more valuable, more just,* than the vulgar wisdom of official liberalism, singing, shouting, invoking, vociferating about the fussiness of revolutionary fuss, about the futility of the revolutionary struggle and the charms of counter-revolutionary 'constitutional' nonsense.[2]

This is how a man could write who knew the spirit, the essence of Marx's teachings: this is how Lenin could write, he who long before the October Revolution saw the victorious path of Marxism. And if after the bankruptcy of the opportunist "Marxists," Marxism has revived with new force, if Marxism to-day rules one-sixth of the globe and shakes the whole of the capitalist world to its very foundations, if the spirit of Marx inspires strikes, armed collisions, the struggle of the unemployed

[1] *Vorwärts,* September 3, 1932.
[2] Lenin, Preface to Correspondence of F. A. Sorge, *Collected Works* (Russian edition), p. 178.

and mass movements of the workers in all capitalist countries, the revolts of the downtrodden and oppressed masses of Indo-China, India and the Black Continent—if the banner of Marxism flutters over Soviet China—it can be explained by the fact that *Marx combined revolutionary theory with revolutionary practice.* Marx knew and included in the armoury of international communism the principle that "without a revolutionary theory there can be no revolutionary movement" (Lenin); that "theory out of touch with revolutionary practice is like a mill without any grist, just as practice gropes in the dark unless revolutionary theory throws a light on the path." [1]

This is why Marx is recorded in the history of the world labour movement not only as a highly gifted theoretician, but as a highly gifted leader and organiser of the working class; this is why we have the right to say that *without revolutionary Marxian theory and without revolutionary practice there neither is nor can there be any revolutionary trade union movement.*

[1] Stalin, *Foundations of Leninism,* III, "Theory."

CHAPTER XI

For Marxism-Leninism in the Trade Union Movement

THE creator of Marxism was as monolithic as his teachings. The British socialist Hyndman in his reminiscences of Marx relates the following: "I remember I once told Marx that as I grew older I became apparently more tolerant. 'More tolerant!' answered Marx—'more tolerant?' It was clear that he was not becoming more tolerant." [1]

This philistine, who went over to the camp of British imperialism, correctly noted the chief feature of Marx. And this is also the chief feature of Marxism. Revolutionary Marxism cannot owing to "age" become more tolerant towards its ideological and political enemies. ⸢The power of revolutionary Marxism consists precisely in its irreconcilability.⸥ This ideological and political irreconcilability of Marxism was taken as the basis of the Bolshevik Party and was the guiding line in the theoretical and political activity of V. I. Lenin, the brilliant pupil of Marx.⸥

Marx laid the foundation of the doctrine concerning trade unions. He defined the *rôle* of the trade unions in the capitalist State, he established a correct relationship between the economic and political struggle, he established the primacy of the political over the economic struggle. Marx indicated the limits and scope of activity of the trade unions, building his trade union tactics on the basis of the revolutionary class struggle, organically linking up the struggle for the workers' immediate demands with the struggle for their ultimate goal. Marx proved that those trade unions which do not struggle against the bourgeoisie merely become a weapon in its hands against the interests of the working class. *Marx defined the past,*

[1] Lenin, *Hyndman on Marx, Collected Works* (Russian edition) Vol. XV, p. 268.

present and future of the trade unions in the capitalist countries.

But Marx could not define the *rôle* of the trade unions after the seizure of power by the working class; he could not state what place the trade unions would occupy under the dictatorship of the proletariat. This was done by the great pupil and follower of Marx, the founder and organiser of the Russian Bolshevik Party—Lenin. Lenin did this basing himself on the theory of Marx. Lenin enriched and developed Marxism on the basis of the experiences acquired in the world labour movement and in a number of revolutions. This is why we say that "Leninism is Marxism in the epoch of imperialism and proletarian revolution." To be more exact—"Leninism is the theory and tactics of the proletarian revolution in general, the theory and tactics of the dictatorship of the proletariat in particular" (Stalin). Lenin theoretically and practically worked on all problems pertaining to the dictatorship of the proletariat and therefore he could not but touch on such an important pillar of the proletarian dictatorship as the trade unions. What is the central, the guiding idea of Lenin on the question of the trade unions? The idea was already formulated by Marx—that the trade unions are schools of communism. This formula, in spite of its brevity, is very rich in content. And, as a matter of fact, four principal ideas are included in this definition: (1) The trade unions are organisations that must embrace the whole class; (2) the trade unions politically educate the masses in the spirit of communism, raising them to the level of understanding their general class tasks; (3) the trade unions link up the Party with the masses, *i.e.,* the vanguard with the class; (4) the trade unions wage the struggle against Capital under the leadership of the revolutionary party of the proletariat.

Some "theoreticians" are perplexed at the formula—"the trade unions are schools of communism," for they take "schools" in the literal sense of the word. The difference between an ordinary school and a trade union is that the trade union is a class school. It collects scattered workers, carries on preliminary work to turn these workers into a class and they are turned into a class *not by knowledge gained from text-books but knowledge gained in class battles*. In the capitalist countries this instruction occurs in the battles against capitalism (strikes,

demonstrations, revolts, or any other form of struggle); in the
U.S.S.R.—in the active participation of the trade unions in the
construction of socialism (participation in the management of
national economy, socialist competition, shock brigades, labour
discipline, raising the material and cultural level of the masses,
etc.). Both in the one case as well as the other, this school is
of a special type, and he who imagines that the trade unions are
ordinary schools is no more than a schoolboy in the problems
of Marxism-Leninism. The question of what the formula "the
trade unions are schools of communism" means seems to be
clear especially to the members of the C.P.S.U. But if we follow
our trade union literature more attentively, we see that there
is confusion in the minds of some "theoreticians." Here, for
example, is what V. Yarotsky writes, who under Comrade
Tomsky was looked upon as a theoretician of the trade union
movement:

> The formula 'Schools of Communism' is incomplete. A
> scientific definition must differentiate the phenomenon defined
> from the chain of cognate phenomena. The formula must be so
> constructed that it covers only the given phenomenon. And this
> is precisely what is missing in the formula 'The unions are schools
> of communism.' Isn't the Communist Party a school of com-
> munism? Doesn't any workers' club in actual fact fulfil the rôle
> of just such a school of communism? The methods of pedagogical
> influence over their members differ in all of these organisations.
> The composition of their membership also varies. *But they are
> all schools of communism, to the same extent as the workers'
> co-operative is.* Thus, the formula 'the trade unions are schools
> of communism' covers, during a certain stage of development
> of the working class, all organisations of the working class. It
> is quite evident that this formula, defining the functions of the
> unions, to a certain extent does not permit us to draw a sharp and
> clear-cut line between the trade unions and other proletarian
> organisations. Evidently, it is inadequate.[1]

"The formula—the trade unions are schools of communism,"
says our theoretician, "is incomplete and inadequate." But
Yarotsky himself, in his explanation of the formula "trade

[1] V. Yarotsky, *History, Theory and Practice of the Trade Union Movement* (Russian edition), Part I. "Nature of Trade Union Movement."
A.U.C.C. T.U. edition, 1925, pp. 31-32.

unions are schools of communism," quotes the words of Lenin: "The trade unions are schools, schools for unification, schools of solidarity, schools for learning how to defend the interests of the workers, schools for learning administration and management." But, it seems, these explanations also do not satisfy our severe "critic." The formula of Lenin is "incomplete and inadequate." Why? Because the "Party is also a school of communism," and the "workers' club" is another such (!) "school of communism," and the "co-operative is a school of communism." We never supposed that the party was—a "school." We, together with Lenin and the Comintern, have been of the opinion up to now that the Russian Bolshevik Party was the vanguard of the working class.

Such anti-Leninist arguments are the result of the complete failure to understand what the Party is. Let us hear what the Second Congress of the Comintern said on this question in the resolution worked out and adopted with the direct participation of Lenin:

> The Communist Party is part of the working class. Namely, its most advanced, intelligent and therefore most revolutionary part. The Communist Party is formed of the best, most intelligent and far-seeing workers. The Communist Party has no other interests than those of the working class. It differs from the general mass of the workers in that it takes a general view of the whole historical march of the working class and at all turns of the road it endeavours to defend the interests, not of separate groups or professions, but of the working class as a whole. The Communist Party is the organised political lever by means of which the more advanced section of the working class leads the whole proletarian and semi-proletarian mass.[1]

This does not sound at all like the childish prattle of Professor Yarotsky who says that the "Party is also a school of Communism." Yarotsky, like all other "critics" of Marxism, confuses the major problems of Marxist-Leninism: the Party, the trade unions and the class.

V. Yarotsky, having stumbled over the formula, "the trade unions are schools of communism," goes to great lengths to

[1] Second Congress of the Comintern, stenographic report (Russian ed.), pp. 368-69. Reprinted as "The Rôle of the Communist Party," Marston Co., London.

M

improve and to complete the definition of a trade union. But, of course, nothing comes of it. Nothing comes of it because his general line is wrong. Here is what Yarotsky recommends in place of the formula of Marx and Lenin:

> The trade union organisation as such is always (?), at all times (?) and in all countries (?) the association of workers best suited to the changing and constantly rising level of class consciousness.[1]

Here we have it, the "universal" formula, "complete" (for all times) (!), all peoples and all countries. The formula is doubtless complete from the point of view of the number of words it contains, but as far as its essence is concerned it is nothing but piffle—thoughtless in content and "scientific" in form. And V. Yarotsky wants us to give up the "incomplete" and "inadequate" formula, "the trade unions are schools of communism," for his high-flown rubbish. Indeed, we cannot accuse him of being too modest. . . . No, we prefer the "incomplete" and "inadequate" formula of Marx-Lenin to a formula replete with nonsense and pretensions (for all times, all peoples, all countries and all trade unions!) such as that of our professor of confusion Yarotsky.

Trotsky too, it will be remembered, began his race back to Social-Democracy with the trade union question. The trade union discussion showed that Trotsky did not and could not understand what the formula "the trade unions are schools of communism" meant, as he monstrously distorted the viewpoint of Marx and Lenin on the rôle of the trade unions, for which he was mercilessly assailed by Lenin, Stalin and the whole Party. In Volume VII of the Lenin *Miscellany*, a pamphlet by Trotsky is published entitled *The Rôle and Tasks of the Trade Unions*, with marginal notes by Lenin to almost every paragraph. Lenin accompanies the arguments given by Trotsky with words like: "Not true, syndicalist trash, blunder, nonsense, etc." These *blunders* with regard to questions of the Party, trade unions and class have led Trotsky straight into the camp of the counter-revolution.

Marx and Lenin, when defining the trade unions, did not

[1] V. Yarotsky, p. 41.

think that *all* trade unions, at all times and in all countries, were schools of communism. They spoke only about those unions *which carry on the class struggle against the capitalists and the capitalist system.* Marx and Lenin could not tolerate people who cover their own theoretical illiteracy with confused "scientific" arguments. We think we have the right to ask: "Is it possible that the trade union movement of the victorious Revolution, the trade union movement that grew out of the teachings of Marx and grew up under the leadership of Lenin, was *even* under Tomsky in need of such 'theories' and such 'theoreticians'?"

The teachings of Lenin on the trade unions actually signify, under new conditions, the application and development of the basic principles of Marx. Lenin (more deeply and better than anyone else) understood the essence and method of Marx and that is why he paid so much attention to the trade union question. Lenin not only continued to develop the theory of the trade union movement (about this we shall speak in a special publication), but he mapped out and defined the strategy and tactics *before, during* and *after* the proletarian revolution. What are the strategy and tactics of Leninism? "The strategy and tactics of Leninism," writes Comrade Stalin, *"constitute the science of leadership of the revolutionary struggle of the proletariat."* [1] And we know that the revolutionary struggle is the principal task of the trade unions. Lenin was the greatest strategist and tactician of the class struggle, precisely because he had completely mastered the method of Marx. Let me give but one example of many that might be cited. In the article intended for Granat's encyclopedia, Lenin writes on the tactics of the proletariat according to Marx:

The fundamental task of proletarian tactics was defined by Marx in strict conformity with the general principles of his materialist-dialectical outlook. Nothing but an objective account of the sum total of all the mutual relationships of all the classes of a given society without exception, and consequently an account of the objective stage of the development of this society as well as an account of the mutual relationships between it and other societies, can serve as the basis for the correct tactics of the class

[1] Stalin, *Problems of Leninism,* "Strategy and Tactics.

that forms the vanguard. All classes and all countries are at the same time looked upon not statically, but dynamically; *i.e.*, not as motionless, but as in motion (the laws of their motion being determined by the economic conditions of existence of each class). The motion in its turn is looked upon not only from the point of view of the past, but also from the point of view of the future; and moreover not only in accordance with the vulgar conception of the 'evolutionists,' who see only slow changes—but dialectically: 'In such great developments—twenty years are as but one day—and there may come days which are the concentrated essence of twenty years,' wrote Marx to Engels (*Briefwechsel*, Vol. III, p. 127). At each stage of development, at each moment, proletarian tactics must take account of these objectively unavoidable dialectics of human history, utilising, on the one hand, the phases of political stagnation, when things are moving at a snail's pace along the road of the so-called 'peaceful' development to increase the class-consciousness, strength and fighting capacity of the most advanced class; on the other hand, conducting this work in the direction of the 'final aim' of the movement of this class, cultivating in it the faculty for the practical performance of great tasks in great days that are the 'concentrated essence of twenty years.' [1]

Only the greatest pupil of Marx and the great master of the proletarian revolution could have defined the tactics of the proletariat as he did here. Lenin proved in practice how it is necessary to act when the "decisive days come, in each of which twenty years may be concentrated."

But Lenin, like Marx, could not foresee everything. Lenin did not and could not give a reply to the question of the *rôle* and the tasks of the trade unions during the reconstruction period. This problem has been worked out and solved by the best pupil of Marx and Lenin, Comrade Stalin. This once more proves that Marxism is not a dogma, is not something set, something fixed once for all time. Marx never understood his teachings and his method metaphysically. Marxism is a live revolutionary science which makes it possible for us to understand the society in which we live and to alter it. It is the "theory and programme of the workers of all countries" (Lenin). Marxism is hostile in the extreme to the theory and

[1] Lenin, *Collected Works*, Vol. XX, Part I. "Teachings of Karl Marx," pp. 42-3. Little Lenin Library No. 1, pp. 32-33.

practice of "Class Harmony"; it has nothing in common with opportunism, which represents "the alliance of a section of the workers with the bourgeoisie against the interests of the proletarian masses" (Lenin). Hence, it follows that only those trade unions which wage the class struggle against the bourgeoisie and its ideological apologists and political helpers and allies have the right to raise aloft the banner of Marxism-Leninism.

· · · · ·

The International Workingmen's Association included in its ranks both political parties and trade unions. Marx's opponents of that day attacked him on two fronts. Some thought that the International Association should accept only trade unions, while others were of the opinion that only political parties should be affiliated to it. But these critics did not understand the significance in principle of *such* a structure of the International Workingmen's Association.

The First International, both in structure and in theory and tactics, stood, thanks to Marx, considerably higher than its constituent parts. It fell apart owing to irreconcilable ideological and political differences and owing to the crushing of the Commune. G. Saidel, an historian of the Second International, thinks otherwise. He writes that the "theoretical dispute between Marx and Bakunin, chiefly on organisational questions (emphasis by G. Saidel), served as the direct cause for the split and demise of the First International." [1] This is not correct. The organisational differences were the result of the *political* differences, and therefore the organisational clashes were not the *cause*, but the occasion for the split. The fall of the Paris Commune dealt an irreparable blow to the First International; "it was an attempt which after the fall of the Paris Commune was no longer feasible in its *first historical form*." [2]

This note of Marx concerning the influence of wars and revolutions, over the fate of international organisations, has been confirmed by history itself. The fall of the Paris Commune led to the falling apart of the First International. The

---

[1] G. Saidel, *Essay on the History of the Second International* (Russian edition), p. 105.
[2] K. Marx, *Critique of the Gotha Programme.*

war of 1914-18 led to the ideological and political bankruptcy of the Socialist and Trade Union Internationals. The October Revolution of 1917 was the impetus for the creation of the Communist International and the Red International of Labour Unions. The First International fell apart *in spite* of the fact that it had occupied a correct position with regard to war and revolution. The Second International fell apart *because* it adhered to the platform of class collaboration, which, when the war began, could not but lead to its disintegration. The Comintern developed and grew and has turned into a great world force on the basis of continuing the revolutionary line of Marx under new conditions, in the epoch of wars and social revolutions. The First International fell apart because its integral parts (the Bakuninists, Blanquists, Proudhonists, trade unionists), were petty-bourgeois socialists and dragged the International from a proletarian policy down to a petty-bourgeois policy.

In spite of the unceasing political and organisational struggle in the ranks of the International Workingmen's Association, the First International was correct in its position that the trade unions must be affiliated to the International Workingmen's Association. At that time it was a necessary prerequisite for the purpose of emphasising the political significance of the trade unions and the necessity of organising them on an international scale.

At the fourth Congress of the First International held in Basle (1869) the following decision was adopted:

> Holding that the international character of labour and capital requires an international organisation of the trade unions, the Congress charges the General Council to bring about an international association of the trade unions.[1]

The First International did not have the opportunity to carry out this decision. When the Second International was established in 1889, the trade unions participated in its congresses, and only a long time afterwards (in 1901) the International Trade Union Secretariat was founded, which became an organisation with equal rights, demonstrating in this way the political

[1] *Handbuch des Sozialismus,* Karl Stegmann & Co., Zurich, 1879, p. 36.

bifurcation of the social-democratic international labour movement. This external bifurcation alongside of internal political
unity aimed at rallying the non-Social-Democratic workers
behind the bourgeoisie under the banner of "neutrality" and
"independence."

The Communist International from the very first days of
its existence followed in the footsteps of the International Workingmen's Association with regard to this question. At the Second
Congress of the Communist International representatives of the
revolutionary trade unions were present, including the Anarcho-
Syndicalist Confederation of Labour of Spain. The statutes
adopted by the Second Congress of the Communist International
read:

> The trade unions who have accepted the Communist platform
> and are united on an international scale under the control of the
> Executive Committee of the Communist International form
> Trade Union Sections of the Communist International. The
> Communist Trade Unions send their representatives to the World
> Congresses of the Communist International through the medium
> of the Communist Parties of their respective countries. The
> Trade Union Sections of the Communist International delegate
> a representative with a decisive vote to the Executive Committee
> of the Communist International. The Executive Committee of
> the Communist International enjoys the right of sending a repre-
> sentative with a decisive vote to the Trade Union Section of the
> Communist International.[1]

This viewpoint of the Comintern, exhibited in a number of
documents even before the Second Congress, served as the beginning of political differentiation in the revolutionary trade
unions. Those trade unions that had been firmly won by the
Communists passed on to the *organisational* crystallisation of
their communist ideas. Thus, the Third Trade Union Congress
of the R.S.F.S.R. (March, 1930), adopted the following resolution on the report concerning the international trade union
movement:

> The struggle of the international proletariat is being waged
> not for reforming capitalism, but for overthrowing it. In this

[1] *Second Congress of the Communist International,* Stenographic Report
(Russian edition), p. 624.

revolutionary struggle all class-conscious revolutionary elements are rallying more and more determinedly to the ranks of the Third International, as the organisation embodying the world proletarian revolution.

The trade unions of Russia, which side by side with the Communist Party fought for the overthrow of capitalism in Russia, cannot remain outside the ranks of the Third International, and therefore the Third Trade Union Congress herewith resolves:

To join the Third Communist International, and to call upon the revolutionary trade unions of all countries to follow the example set by the Russian proletariat organised in trade unions.[1]

Such a decision could have been adopted only by the most advanced trade union movement, led and guided by the tested Bolshevik Party. Among the revolutionary trade unions of the capitalist countries, which then only began to crystallise out of the reformist and anarcho-syndicalist trade union movement, the decision of the Second Congress was looked upon as belittling the *rôle* of the trade unions. The anarcho-syndicalists, who during that period came to us, began to experience difficulties under the blows of the anarchists, who interpreted the decision of the Comintern as the abolition of the organisational independence of the trade unions, etc. It was quite evident that the decision on the direct affiliation of the trade unions to the Comintern, which was correct in principle and corresponded to the traditions of the First International, was *premature,* and might have delayed for some time the development of the trade union movement in the capitalist countries towards the Communist International. When the Unitary Confederation of Labour of France in 1922 made it a condition of its affiliation to the R.I.L.U. that the mutual representation between the Executive of the Comintern and the R.I.L.U. be abolished, we, on the advice of Lenin, made this concession, emphasising in our declaration that we adhered to the position of the leading *rôle* of the Comintern with regard to the Red International of Labour Unions.

Experience has shown that it is better to carry out a correct policy through a Communist fraction than through the mutual representation as provided for in the statutes. However, the

[1] *Resolutions and Decisions of the Third All-Russian Trade Union Congress* (Russian edition), 1920, p. 47.

question of principle which had been raised by the structure and principles of the International Workingmen's Association remained: Shall the revolutionary trade unions in future affiliate to the Communist International, or is this inadmissible on principle? To this question there can be but one answer: emphatically yes.

Building a revolutionary International of such a type does not mean fusing the Party and the trade unions, nor does it mean the merger of the Party and the trade unions, but only the synthesis of these *two* forms of the labour movement in a single International. I emphasise—*two* and not *all* forms of the labour movement, because with the victory of the October Revolution the old "classical" division of the labour movement into three forms (the Party, trade unions and the co-operatives) had clearly outlived its day.

"The proletarian revolution in Russia has brought forward the fundamental form of the workers' dictatorship—the soviets. The new divisions which are now everywhere forming are: (1) Party, (2) Soviet, and (3) Industrial Union." [1] The victory of the proletarian revolution does not do away with the old problem— the Party, the trade unions and the class—but raises this problem in a new light. Whereas the trade unions must unite "every single member of the proletariat" (Lenin), the Party during the whole of the transition period unites in its ranks only the vanguard, *i.e.*, its most advanced and most class-conscious section. To raise during the transition period the question of fusing the Party and the trade unions would mean to raise the question of fusing the Party and the class, *i.e.*, of merging the Party in the class, would mean the disappearance of the Party, which is absolutely inconceivable without the abolition of classes and the establishment of complete communism throughout the whole world. This same resolution of the Second Congress of the Comintern, a resolution *amended and supplemented by Lenin*, says the following on the subject:

The necessity of a political party for the proletariat can cease only with the complete abolition of classes. On the way to this

[1] Resolution on *The Rôle of the Communist Party in the Proletarian Revolution*. Stenographic Report of the Second Congress of the Communist International, 1920 edition, p. 42.

final victory of communism it is possible that the relative importance of the three fundamental proletarian organisations of modern times (Party, Soviets and Industrial Union) may undergo some change; and that gradually *a single type of workers' organisation will be formed*. The Communist Party, however, will become absorbed in the working class only when *Communism ceases to be the object of struggle,* and the whole working class shall have become Communist.[1]

For this reason the question of fusing the Party and the trade unions must not be raised now, while at a definite stage the question of forming a *single* International will be raised.

The Communist International grew parallel with the growth of the U.S.S.R. and the development of the revolutionary international labour movement. In proportion as the Comintern and the R.I.L.U. will wrest the masses away from international reformism, as the forces of the international proletariat will continue to rally under the banner of communism, the contacts between the Comintern and the international revolutionary trade union movement will grow and strengthen. Thereby the conditions for the existence of *one* revolutionary International will be created. In this way, at a certain stage of the struggle, the R.I.L.U. can become also *organisationally* a part of the Communist International.

These prospects are not simply figments of the imagination but are based on the general tendencies of development of world politics, world economics and the world labour movement. They are based on our firm and unshakable *scientific* conviction that the final and permanent victory of Marxism-Leninism the world over will come.

Our entire policy, strategy and tactics proceed from the following thesis of Lenin as their point of departure: *The doctrine of Marx is all-powerful because it is correct.*

[1] Resolution on *The Rôle of the Communist Party in the Proletarian Revolution,* Stenographic Report of the Second Congress of the Communist International, 1920 edition, p. 44.

INDEX